Wonders

Reading/Writing Companion

McGraw Hill

mheducation.com/prek-12

Copyright © 2023 McGraw Hill

Send all inquiries to:
McGraw Hill
1325 Avenue of the Americas
New York, NY 10019

ISBN: 978-1-26-574898-2
MHID: 1-26-574898-5

Printed in the United States of America.

3 4 5 6 7 8 9 LMN 26 25 24 23 22   A

Welcome to WONDERS!

We're here to help you set goals to build on the amazing things you already know. We'll also help you reflect on everything you'll learn.

Let's start by taking a look at the incredible things you'll do this year.

You'll build knowledge on exciting topics and find answers to interesting questions.

You'll read fascinating fiction, informational texts, and poetry and respond to what you read with your own thoughts and ideas.

And you'll research and write stories, poems, and essays of your own!

Here's a sneak peek at how you'll do it all.

"Let's go!"

You'll explore new ideas by reading groups of different texts about the same topic. These groups of texts are called *text sets*.

At the beginning of a text set, we'll help you set goals on the My Goals page. You'll see a bar with four boxes beneath each goal. Think about what you already know to fill in the bar. Here's an example.

I can read and understand narrative nonfiction.

As you move through a text set, you'll explore an essential question and build your knowledge of a topic until you're ready to write about it yourself.

You'll also learn skills that will help you reach your text set goals. At the end of lessons, you'll see a new Check In bar with four boxes.

CHECK IN 1 2 3 4

Reflect on how well you understood a lesson to fill in the bar.

Here are some questions you can ask yourself.

- Was I able to complete the task?

- Was it easy, or was it hard?

- Do I think I need more practice?

You have plenty of tools and resources to learn more, such as anchor charts and center activities. You can also reread a lesson or ask a teacher or peer for help.

It's okay if I think I need more practice. The most important thing is that I do my best and keep learning!

Thinking about what works best for me will help me choose what to do next.

At the end of each text set, you'll show off the knowledge you built by completing a fun task. Then you'll return to the second My Goals page where we'll help you reflect on all that you learned.

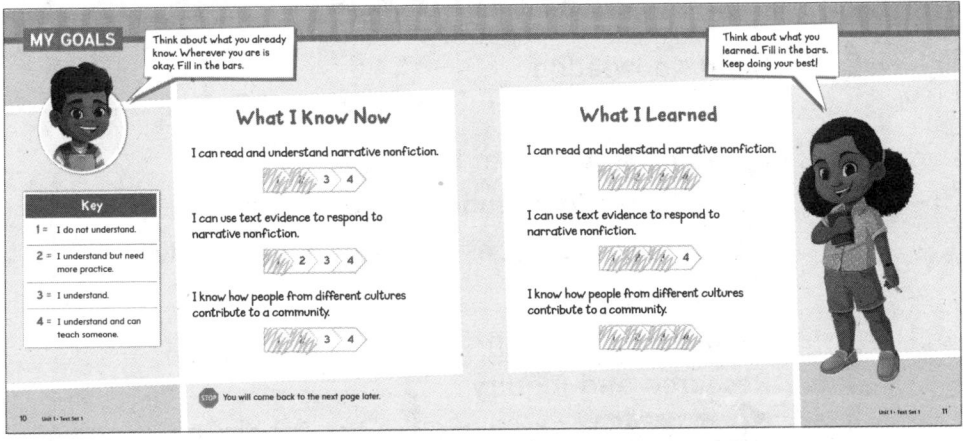

I'll fill in a new set of bars to show how far I've come. I started at 2, but now I'm at 4 because I can read and understand narrative nonfiction well enough to teach a friend.

I'll follow the same steps as I write my own stories, essays, and poems. I own my learning, and you can own yours!

"Let's get started!"

TEXT SET 3 **ARGUMENTATIVE TEXT**

EXTENDED WRITING

CONNECT AND REFLECT

Digital Tools

Find this eBook and other resources at **my.mheducation.com**

TEXT SET 1 **EXPOSITORY TEXT**

TEXT SET 2 **HISTORICAL FICTION**

TEXT SET 3 **POETRY**

EXTENDED WRITING

CONNECT AND REFLECT

 Digital Tools

Find this eBook and
other resources at
my.mheducation.com

Build Knowledge

? Essential Question

How do people from different cultures contribute to a community?

Build Vocabulary

Write new words you learned about people, cultures, and communities. Draw lines and circles for the words you write.

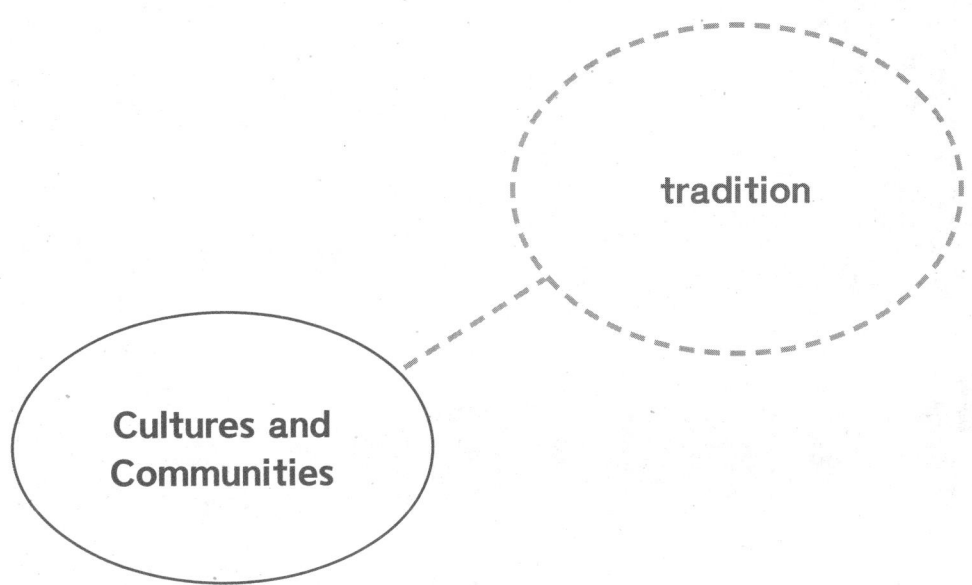

tradition

Cultures and Communities

Go online to **my.mheducation.com** and read the "Who Made That?" Blast. Think about why learning about other cultures is important. Then blast back your response.

Think about what you already know. Wherever you are is okay. Fill in the bars.

What I Know Now

I can read and understand narrative nonfiction.

1 > 2 > 3 > 4

I can use text evidence to respond to narrative nonfiction.

1 > 2 > 3 > 4

I know how people from different cultures contribute to a community.

1 > 2 > 3 > 4

Key	
1 =	I do not understand.
2 =	I understand but need more practice.
3 =	I understand.
4 =	I understand and can teach someone.

STOP You will come back to the next page later.

Think about what you learned. Fill in the bars. Keep doing your best!

What I Learned

I can read and understand narrative nonfiction.

1 > 2 > 3 > 4

I can use text evidence to respond to narrative nonfiction.

1 > 2 > 3 > 4

I know how people from different cultures contribute to a community.

1 > 2 > 3 > 4

SHARED READ

My Goal I can read and understand narrative nonfiction.

TAKE NOTES

As you read, make note of interesting words and important events.

Room to Grow

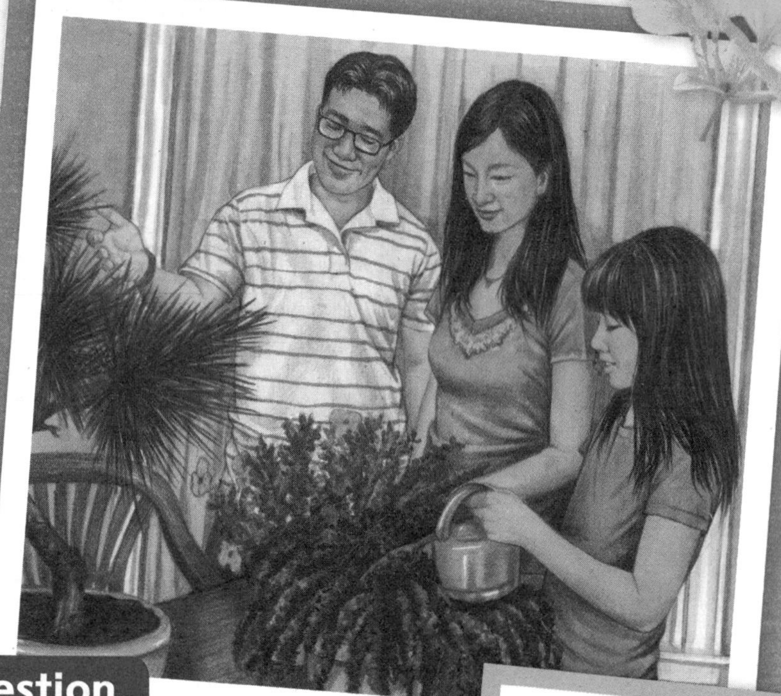
Our new home in Portland

Essential Question

How do people from different cultures contribute to a community?

Read how one family helps their community grow.

Spring in the City

My name is Kiku Sato. Last spring, my family and I moved from the country to the big city.

Our new home in Portland had no yard. There wasn't even a tiny plot of land. So Mama made an indoor garden. First she and Papa planted seeds in pots. Then they hung them from hooks. Next they crammed plants onto shelves. Green vines **tumbled** over desks. Soon our house had plants everywhere.

At first, I was **scared** to start school. I was afraid no one would be my friend. But I soon met a **classmate**. Jill Hernandez and I were **practicing** reading aloud one day. She helped me say her last name, and I helped her **pronounce** mine. The next day we were best friends. Jill spent lots of time at my house.

A map of Oregon

OREGON

PENDLETON

PORTLAND

SALEM

EUGENE

ASHLAND

KEY
- CITY
- ★ CAPITAL
- RIVER

Left & right: (flowers)JAPACK/amanaimagesRF/amanaimages/Corbis; (paper) Wetzel & Company

FIND TEXT EVIDENCE

Read

Paragraphs 1–2

Ask and Answer Questions

Why do Mama and Papa grow an indoor garden? **Circle** text evidence to answer.

Paragraph 3

Chronology

Underline what happens after Kiku meets Jill. What happens the next day?

_____

_____

_____

Maps

Look at the map. **Draw a box around** where Kiku lives.

Reread

Author's Craft

Reread the first paragraph. How do you know who is telling the story?

Paragraph 1

Headings

Draw a box around the heading. How does Jill feel about Mama and Papa's indoor garden?

_____

_____

Circle text evidence.

Paragraph 2

Chronology

What does Mama do before she adds hot water to the tea bowl? **Underline** the text evidence.

Write two signal words here.

_____

_____

Reread

Author's Craft

How does the illustration help you understand the text?

An Idea for a Garden

One afternoon, Jill and her mother came to visit Mama and Papa and me. First they saw our beautiful potted plants. Jill's mother said, "Jill **admires** your indoor garden. She has told me so much about it."

We all sat down while Mama served tea. First she put green tea into the tea bowl. Then she added hot water and stirred. She handed the bowl to Jill's mother and bowed.

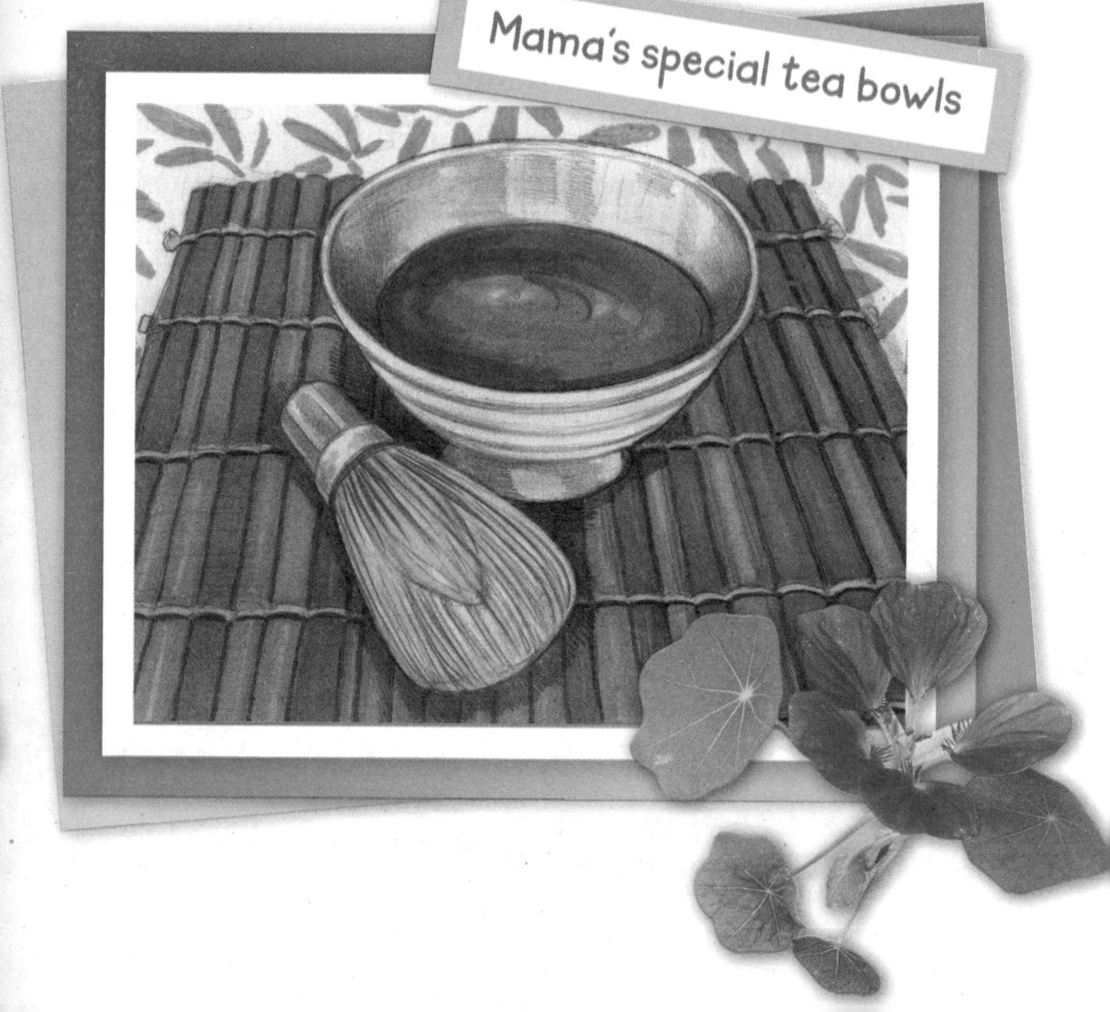

Mama's special tea bowls

Grandmother in Japan

Left & right: (flowers)JAPACK/amanaimagesRF/amanaimages/Corbis; (paper)Wetzel & Company

"My mother taught me how to make tea," said Mama. "She also taught me how to plant a traditional Japanese garden. I learned to make the most of a small, compact space."

All of a sudden, Jill's mother smiled. "Can you help us with a project?" she asked. "Our **community** wants to plant a garden. Our plot is very small. There is so much we want to grow."

Papa looked at Mama, and they both bowed.

"Yes," they said.

FIND TEXT EVIDENCE

Read

Paragraph 1

Ask and Answer Questions

Think of a question about Kiku's grandmother. Write it here.

_____

_____

_____

Underline text evidence that answers your question.

Paragraphs 2–4

Chronology

Circle what happens after Jill's mother asks Mama and Papa to help with the community garden project.

Synthesize Information

Why does Jill's mother ask Kiku's mother for help? **Draw a box around** the text evidence.

Read

Paragraph 1

Chronology

Underline two things that happen in order. Write the signal words that tell when they happen.

_____

_____

_____

Paragraph 2

Compound Words

Circle a compound word. Write what it means.

_____

_____

_____

Reread

Author's Craft

Why is "A Garden Grows" a good heading for this section?

A Garden Grows

First we had a meeting with the community. Everyone agreed to **contribute**. Some people brought seeds, tools, and dirt. Then the next day we met and started our garden.

Papa built long, open boxes. Next, we filled them with dirt. The tallest box went close to the back wall. The boxes got shorter and shorter. The shortest box was in the front. "All the plants will get sunlight without making shade for the others," Mama said.

Papa builds boxes

Jill and I plant seeds

Then, we used round, flat stones to make a rock path. Papa said that in Japan, stones are an important part of a garden. Finally, we planted the seeds.

Jill and I worked in the garden all summer. Our community grew many different vegetables. At the end of the summer, we picked enough vegetables to have a cookout. Mama brought a big pot of miso and vegetable stew. Everyone thanked Mama and Papa for their help. They brought a bit of Japan to Portland. I was so proud.

Look what we picked!

Summarize

Use your notes and think about what happens in "Room to Grow." Summarize the text using the order of events.

NARRATIVE NONFICTION

FIND TEXT EVIDENCE

Read

Paragraph 1
Chronology
Underline what happens after Papa makes the rock path. Write the signal word here.

_____

Paragraph 2
Ask and Answer Questions
Write a question about the cookout.

_____

_____

_____

_____

Reread

Author's Craft

How does the author help you understand how everyone feels about Mama and Papa?

Vocabulary

Use the sentences to talk with a partner about each word. Then answer the questions. Respond with your new vocabulary. It will help you remember the meaning of the words.

admires

My family **admires** my good test grades.

What do you admire about a friend?

_____

classmate

Don and his **classmate** Maria always eat lunch together.

What things do you do with a classmate?

_____

> **Build Your Word List** Reread the first paragraph on page 16. Draw a box around the word _meeting_. In your reader's notebook, use a word web to write more forms of the word. Use a dictionary.

community

Many people in my **community** work together.

What do you like about your community?

_____

_____

contribute

Mom will **contribute** clothes to people who can use them.

What is something you can contribute?

_____

_____

practicing

Kyle has been **practicing**, and now he can play lots of songs.

What skill can you improve by practicing?

_____

_____

pronounce

Cindy can **pronounce** her name in another language.

How can you learn how to pronounce new words?

_____

_____

scared

Our dog hides during storms because he is **scared**.

What do you do when you feel scared?

_____

_____

tumbled

The ripe tomatoes **tumbled** out of the big basket onto the ground.

What does *tumbled* mean?

_____

_____

Compound Words

A compound word is made up of two smaller words joined together. Use the meanings of the two smaller words, or base words, to help you figure out what the compound word means.

FIND TEXT EVIDENCE

I see the compound word afternoon *on page 14. It has two smaller words,* after *and* noon. *I know what* after *means. I know* noon *means "12 o'clock." I think* afternoon *means "after 12 o'clock."*

One afternoon, Jill and her mother came to visit.

Your Turn Figure out the meaning of the compound word.

cookout, page 17 _____

CHECK IN ⟩ 1 ⟩ 2 ⟩ 3 ⟩ 4 ⟩

Ask and Answer Questions

Ask yourself questions as you read to check your understanding of a text. Then look for details to support your answers.

 **FIND TEXT EVIDENCE**
Look at the section "Spring in the City" on page 13. Think of a question, and then read to answer it.

Page 13

Spring in the City

My name is Kiku Sato. Last spring, my family and I moved from the country to the big city.

Our new home in Portland had no yard. There wasn't even a tiny plot of land. So Mama made an indoor garden. First she and Papa planted seeds in pots. Then they hung them from hooks. Next they crammed plants onto shelves. Green vines **tumbled** over desks. Soon our house had plants everywhere.

I have a question. Why were there so many plants in Kiku's house? I read that they did not have a yard. I also read that Mama and Papa planted lots of seeds indoors. I can answer my question. Kiku's family likes to grow plants but didn't have space outdoors.

Your Turn Reread the first paragraph on page 17. Think of one question. You might ask: *Why did Kiku's father use round, flat stones in the garden?* With a partner, reread the section to find text evidence. Then write the answer here.

_____

_____

> **Quick Tip**
>
> Asking questions helps you understand the text better. As you read, stop and ask yourself questions. Then reread to find text evidence.

CHECK IN 1 2 3 4

Headings and Maps

"Room to Grow" is an **autobiography**. An autobiography

- is a kind of narrative nonfiction
- tells the true story of a person's life in time order
- is written by that person and uses the pronouns *I* and *me*
- may use text features, such as headings and maps

🔍 FIND TEXT EVIDENCE

"Room to Grow" is an autobiography. It is a true story by Kiku about her life. I see time-order words and the pronouns I and me. Kiku uses headings and a map to add meaning to the story.

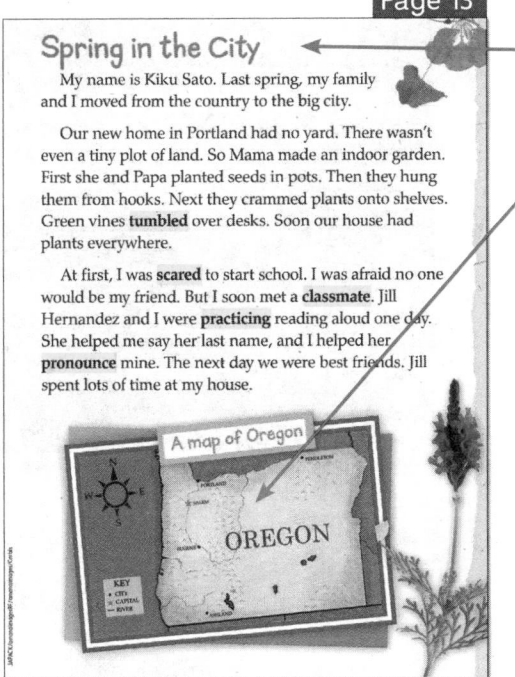

Page 13

Spring in the City

My name is Kiku Sato. Last spring, my family and I moved from the country to the big city.

Our new home in Portland had no yard. There wasn't even a tiny plot of land. So Mama made an indoor garden. First she and Papa planted seeds in pots. Then they hung them from hooks. Next they crammed plants onto shelves. Green vines **tumbled** over desks. Soon our house had plants everywhere.

At first, I was **scared** to start school. I was afraid no one would be my friend. But I soon met a **classmate**. Jill Hernandez and I were **practicing** reading aloud one day. She helped me say her last name, and I helped her **pronounce** mine. The next day we were best friends. Jill spent lots of time at my house.

A map of Oregon

OREGON

KEY
· CITY
⭐ CAPITAL
— RIVER

Headings
A heading tells what a section of text is mostly about.

Maps
A map is a flat drawing of a real place.

COLLABORATE

Your Turn Look at the map on page 13. What is something you learned from the map that isn't in the main text of the selection?

_____

_____

CHECK IN　1　2　3　4

Chronology

Chronology, or time order, is the order in which events take place. Certain words, called signal words, show the order of events. Look for words such as *first, next, before, then, soon,* and *finally.*

🔍 FIND TEXT EVIDENCE

In "Room to Grow," the events are told in the order they happened. I see the signal word first *in "Spring in the City" on page 13. I will read to find out what happens next. I will look for signal words to help me.*

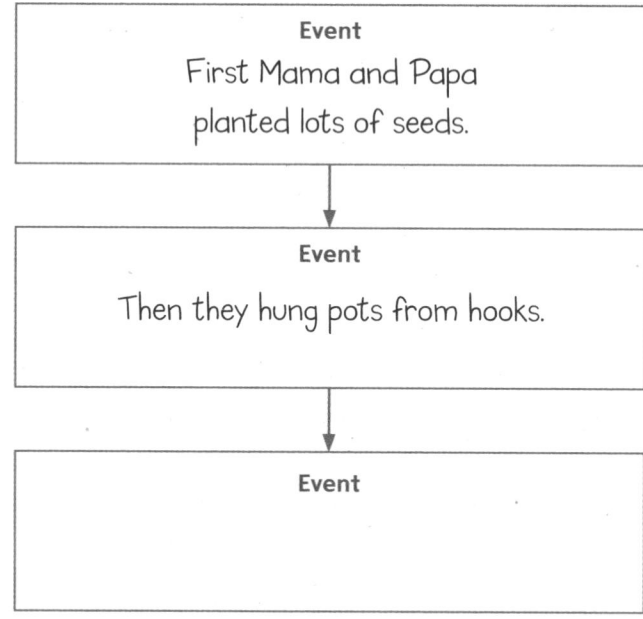

Event
First Mama and Papa planted lots of seeds.

↓

Event
Then they hung pots from hooks.

↓

Event

 **Your Turn** Reread page 16. How do Kiku and her family help plant the garden? List the events in order in your graphic organizer.

COLLABORATE

CHECK IN ⟩ 1 ⟩ 2 ⟩ 3 ⟩ 4 ⟩

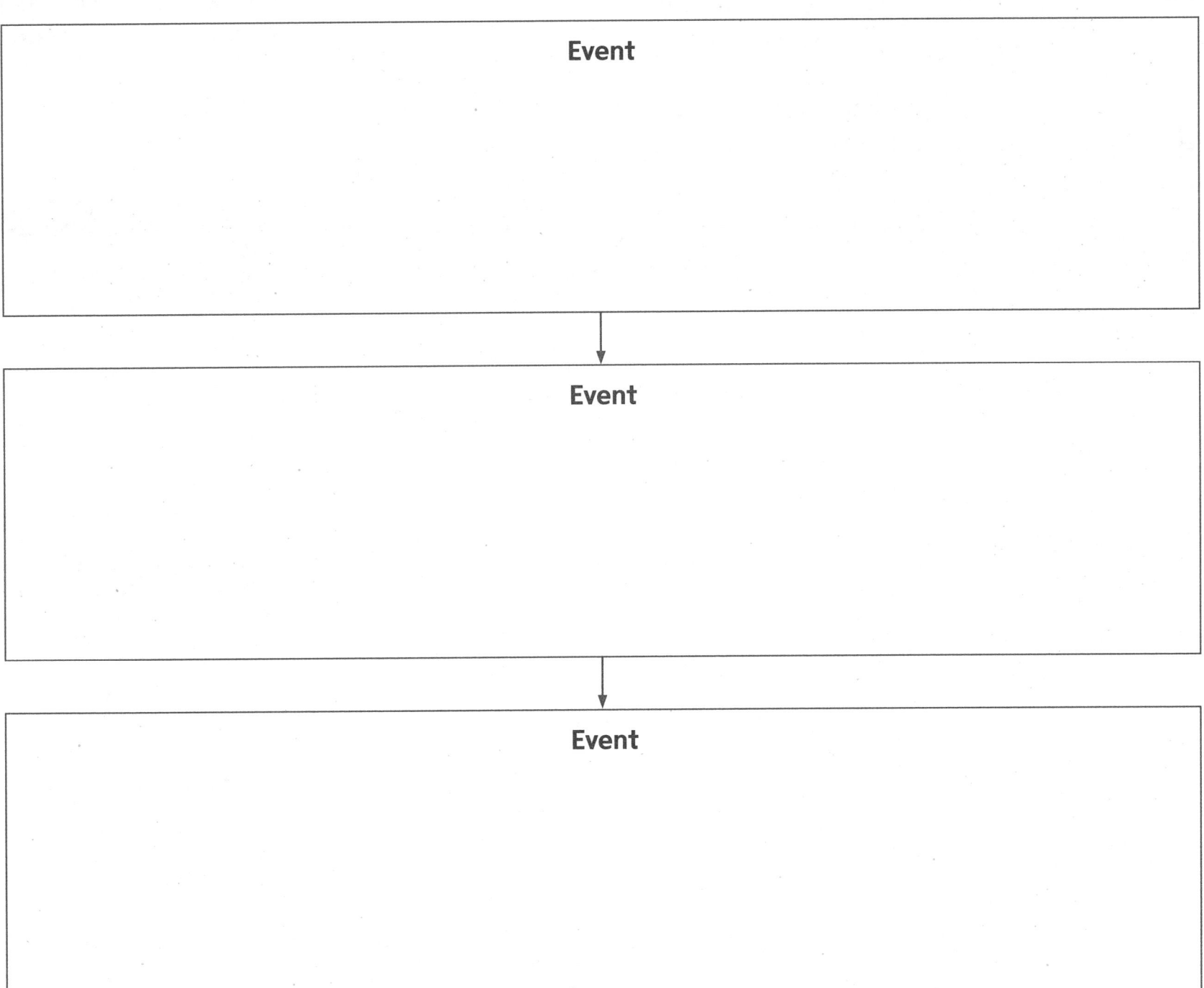

Event

Event

Event

My Goal I can use text evidence to respond to narrative nonfiction.

Respond to Reading

Talk about the prompt below. Use your notes and evidence from the text to support your answer.

How do Mama and Papa help Kiku feel proud of who she is?

_____

_____

_____

_____

_____

_____

_____

_____

Quick Tip

Use these sentence starters to talk about the prompt.

One thing Mama and Papa do is . . .

Kiku feels proud because . . .

Grammar Connections

As you write your response, be sure to check that you have capitalized the names of people and the places they live. Remember to write complete sentences.

CHECK IN 1 > 2 > 3 > 4

Culture in Your Community

COLLABORATE

Every community has places that show its culture. Follow the research process to make a map that shows some of these places in your community. Work with a partner.

Step 1 **Set a Goal** Make a list of places you want to include on your map. _____

Step 2 **Identify Sources** Use books, magazines, and websites to find information about your community and its culture.

Step 3 **Find and Record Information** Find information in your sources and take notes. Cite your sources.

Step 4 **Organize and Combine Information** Organize your information by sorting the places you found into groups. Decide on a symbol to represent each group. Make a rough sketch of your map.

Step 5 **Create and Present** Create a final map. Think about how you will present your map to the class.

Quick Tip

Parks, libraries, museums, statues, stores, and restaurants are some of the places that show a community's culture.

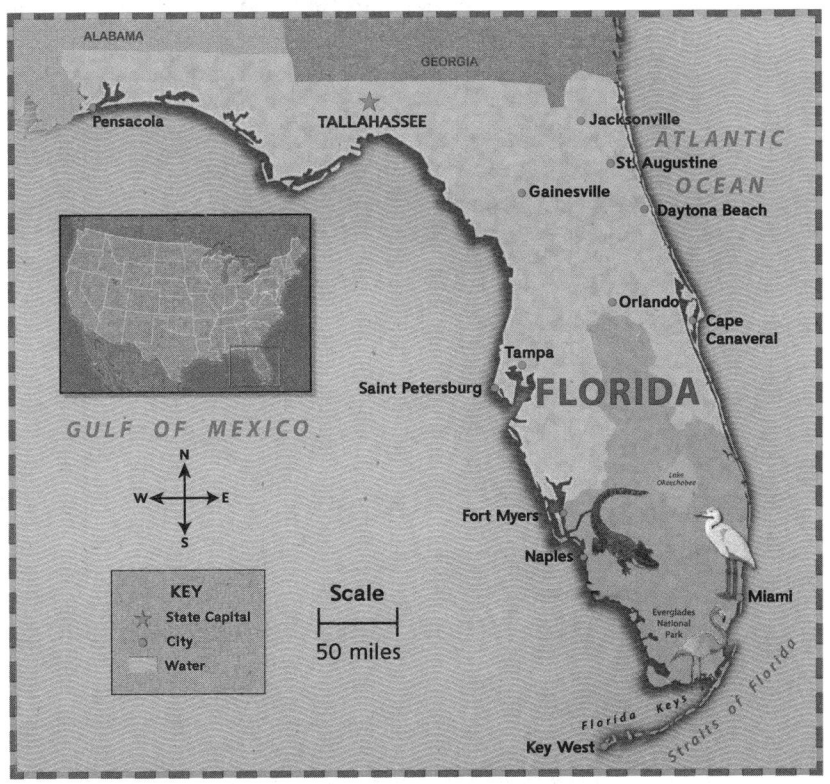

CHECK IN 1 2 3 4

Gary the Dreamer

Literature Anthology:
pages 10–21

? **How is knowing what Gary did as a child important to understanding his autobiography?**

Talk About It Reread **Literature Anthology** page 13. Talk with a partner about how Gary played when he was a child.

Cite Text Evidence What words and phrases help you picture how Gary played? Write text evidence in the chart.

Text Evidence	What It Tells About Gary

Make Inferences

An inference is a conclusion based on facts. For example, Gary dreams about making a touchdown, so he must like football. What can you infer about why Gary's childhood is important?

Write I know Gary's childhood is important because it

shows that _____

_____

_____

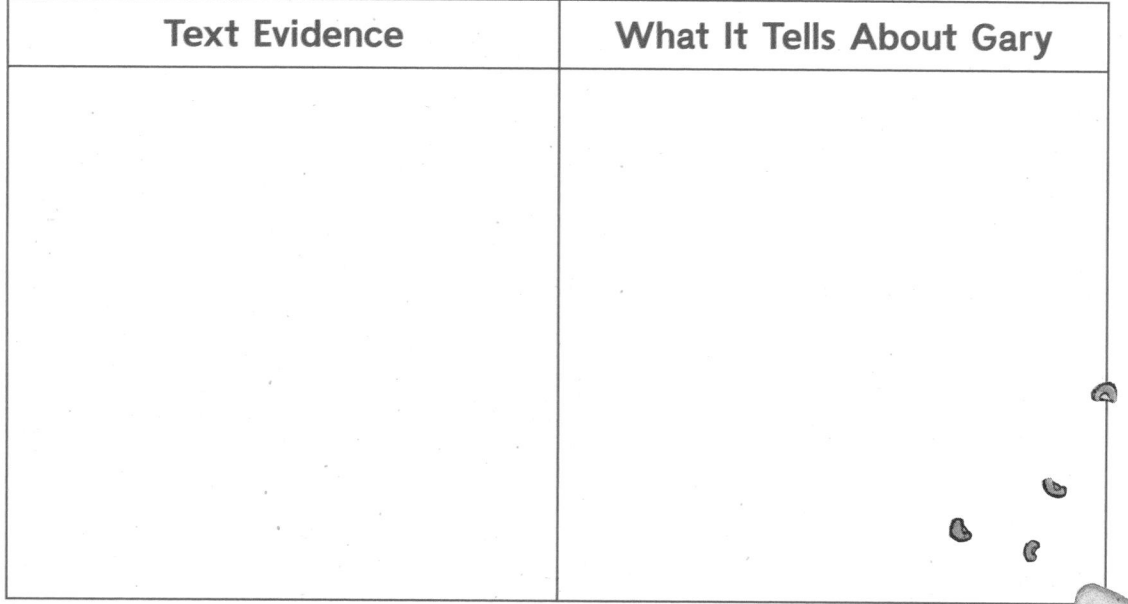

CHECK IN 〉 1 〉 2 〉 3 〉 4 〉

How does the author help you learn more about his character?

Talk About It Look at **Literature Anthology** pages 14 and 15. Talk about what you see and what it tells about Gary.

Cite Text Evidence How is Gary different from his classmates? Write text evidence and explain how you know.

Gary	His Classmates	How I Know

Write Gary Soto helps me know more about his life by _____

_____

_____

Quick Tip

I can use these sentence starters to talk about Gary.

I read that . . .

I can use the illustration to . . .

Combine Information

Make a connection between what you already know and what you read about Gary Soto to create a new understanding. Talk about what Gary wants you to know and why.

CHECK IN 1 2 3 4

Why is *Gary the Dreamer* a good title for this story?

Talk About It Reread **Literature Anthology** page 21. Talk about how Gary Soto uses the word *dreamed*.

Cite Text Evidence How does Gary use the word *dreamed* to show how he has changed? Write text evidence in the diagram.

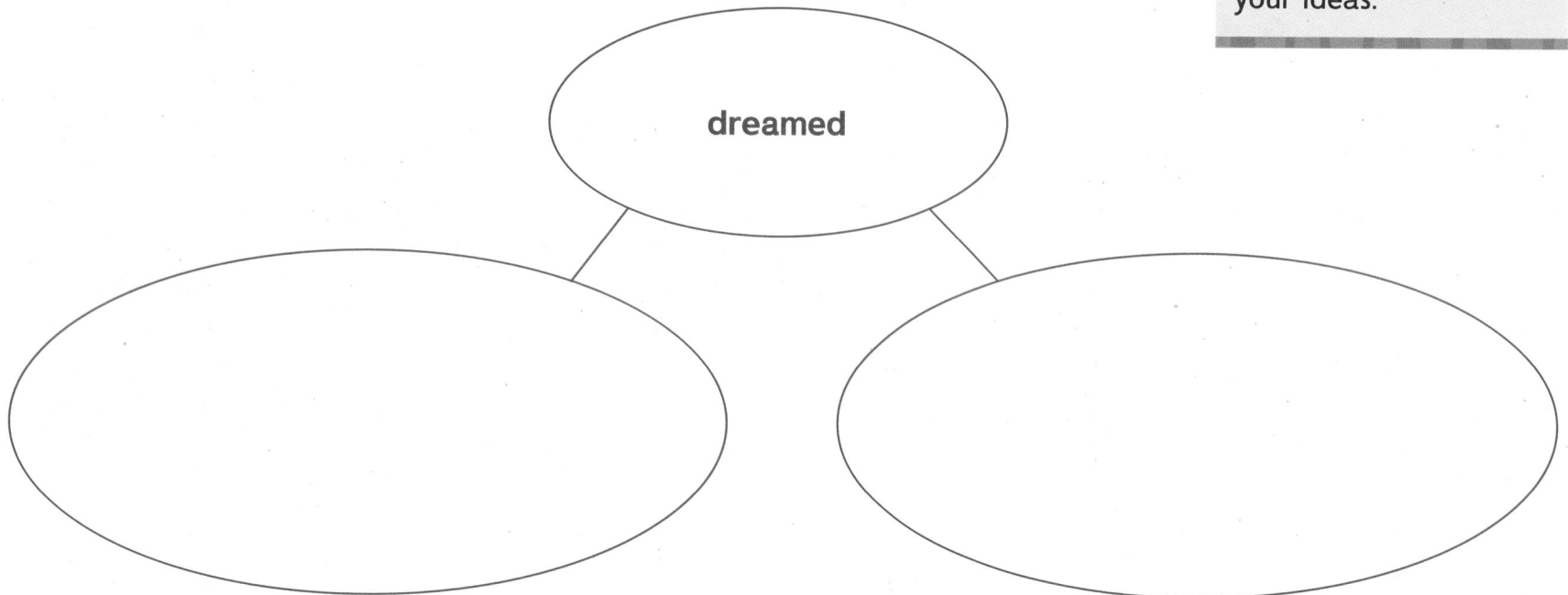

dreamed

Write *Gary the Dreamer* is a good title for this story because it

tells me that _____

_____

CHECK IN 1 2 3 4

Respond to Reading

COLLABORATE Talk about the prompt below. Use your notes and text evidence to support your answer.

How did Gary Soto's dreams help him become a writer?

_____

_____

_____

_____

_____

_____

_____

_____

_____

_____

Quick Tip

Use these sentence starters to talk about Gary Soto.

One thing Gary dreamed about is . . .

Gary's dreams show he is . . .

This helped him as a writer because . . .

CHECK IN 1 2 3 4

Sharing Cultures

Pat Mora Loves Books

[1]   Pat Mora has a special word for how she feels about books. She calls it *bookjoy*. Born in El Paso, Texas, in 1942, Pat learned to love books and reading from her mother. Books are magic to Pat.

[2]   "I wouldn't be me without books," she says.

[3]   Pat grew up in a bilingual home. That means she and her family spoke both English and Spanish. Pat is proud of her culture. She has written more than 36 children's books. Many of them are written in both English and Spanish.

[4]   Pat uses her stories and poems to share her culture. She works hard to share her love of books with all children. Every year in April, many libraries and schools in America celebrate Día. Día is the nickname for Children's Day, Book Day. *Día* means "day" in Spanish. Children get together at libraries, schools, and parks to celebrate. It's like a big book fiesta, or party.

Literature Anthology:
pages 24–25

Reread and use the prompts to take notes in the text.

Reread paragraphs 1 and 2. How does the author help you understand how Pat Mora feels about books? **Underline** text evidence.

COLLABORATE

Reread paragraphs 3 and 4. Talk with a partner about how Pat Mora shares her culture with others. **Circle** text evidence.

Remember to take turns speaking when you work with a partner. Try to stay on topic. Speak clearly and pay attention to what your partner says.

Anna Kucherova/Shutterstock.com

Heroes and History

[5]   Kadir Nelson was born in Washington, DC, in 1974. When he was three years old, he picked up a pencil and started drawing. Then, when he turned eleven, he spent the summer with his uncle. His uncle was an artist and teacher. Kadir says that summer changed his life.

[6]   Kadir is inspired by brave and honest leaders. He sometimes paints African American heroes he admires, such as Martin Luther King Jr. He also paints great athletes and everyday heroes, such as dads taking their children to the beach.

[7]   Kadir wants people to feel good when they look at his art. His paintings are colorful and real. They burst with action. Kadir says he has always been an artist. Sharing how he sees the world is part of who he is.

Reread paragraphs 5 and 6. How does the author help you understand how Kadir felt about spending the summer with his uncle?

_____

_____

Circle two details that support your answer.

Reread paragraph 7. How does the author help you visualize Kadir's paintings? **Underline** text evidence.

COLLABORATE

Turn and talk with a partner about the heading. Why is "Heroes and History" a good heading for this section? **Draw a box around** text evidence. Write your answer here.

_____

_____

_____

How does the author use words and phrases to help you visualize how people share their cultures?

 **Talk About It** Reread pages 30 and 31. Talk with a partner about how Pat Mora and Kadir Nelson share their cultures.

Cite Text Evidence What words and phrases help you picture how people share their cultures? Write three ways and how they help.

Quick Tip

When you reread, look for words and phrases that help you picture in your mind what people are doing. Making images in your mind helps you understand the text better.

Text Evidence	How It Helps

Write I can visualize how people share their cultures because

_____

_____

CHECK IN 1 2 3 4

Author's Purpose

An author's purpose is his or her reason for writing. In an expository text, the author's purpose is usually to inform the reader. An author can better inform the reader by using strong, clear language that helps the reader understand the topic.

FIND TEXT EVIDENCE

In "Sharing Cultures" on **Literature Anthology** page 24, the author uses the word *bilingual* to inform the reader about Pat Mora's culture. This helps the reader understand that Pat Mora grew up in a home where two languages were spoken.

> Pat grew up in a bilingual home. That means she and her family spoke both English and Spanish.

Your Turn Reread paragraph 7 on page 31.

- What words does the author use to describe Kadir's art?

  _____

- How do these words help the author inform the reader?

  _____

CHECK IN ⟩ 1 ⟩ 2 ⟩ 3 ⟩ 4 ⟩

? **How is the reason the artist painted this mural the same as the reason Gary Soto wrote *Gary the Dreamer*?**

Talk About It With a partner, talk about the people you see in the mural. Look closely at what each worker does and how the artist shows how each person feels.

Cite Text Evidence Read the caption. Then **circle** three people in the mural. Write what they do in the margin next to them. In the caption, **underline** clues that help you figure out why the artist painted his mural.

Write Connect how the mural artist and Gary Soto use their art and stories to share their love and

pride for their cultures. _____

_____

_____

_____

The artist painted this mural on a building in Chicago, Illinois. He painted real people. The mural celebrates the community's hardworking Latin American people.

CHECK IN 1 2 3 4

Write a Blog Entry

Think about the texts you read that describe how people share their cultures. Why is it important for people from different cultures to contribute to a community? Use text evidence to support your ideas.

1. Look at your Build Knowledge notes in your reader's notebook.

2. Write a blog entry about why it's important for people from different cultures to contribute to a community. Be sure to use examples from the texts you read. Tell your readers how you feel. Use new vocabulary words you have learned in your writing.

3. Write a title for your blog. Draw a picture to go along with what you wrote.

Think about what you learned in this text set. Fill in the bars on page 11.

Build Knowledge

Essential Question

What can traditions teach you about cultures?

Build Vocabulary

 Write new words you learned about cultures and traditions. Draw lines and circles for the words you write.

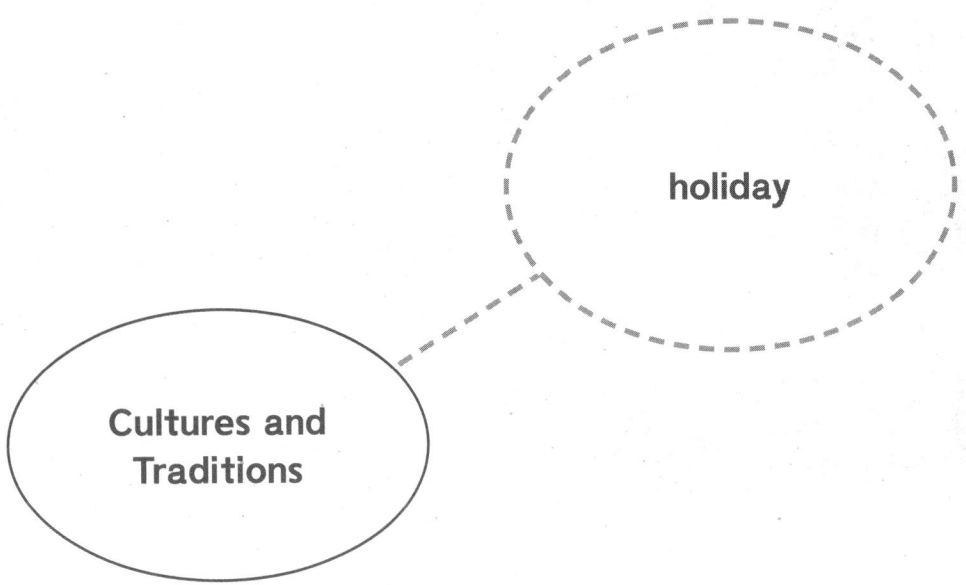

holiday

Cultures and Traditions

 Go online to **my.mheducation.com** and read the "City of Cultures" Blast. Think about why learning about different cultures is important. Then blast back your response.

MY GOALS

Think about what you already know. Fill in the bars. There are no wrong answers here.

What I Know Now

I can read and understand realistic fiction.

| 1 | 2 | 3 | 4 |

Key

1 = I do not understand.

2 = I understand but need more practice.

3 = I understand.

4 = I understand and can teach someone.

I can use text evidence to respond to realistic fiction.

| 1 | 2 | 3 | 4 |

I know how traditions can teach us about cultures.

| 1 | 2 | 3 | 4 |

STOP You will come back to the next page later.

Think about what you learned. Fill in the bars. What helped you the most?

What I Learned

I can read and understand realistic fiction.

| 1 | 2 | 3 | 4 |

I can use text evidence to respond to realistic fiction.

| 1 | 2 | 3 | 4 |

I know how traditions can teach us about cultures.

| 1 | 2 | 3 | 4 |

My Goal I can read and understand realistic fiction.

TAKE NOTES

As you read, make note of interesting words and important events.

_____

_____

_____

_____

_____

_____

_____

_____

_____

The Dream Catcher

Essential Question

? **What can traditions teach you about cultures?**

Read how Peter learns about his culture.

eter walked home from school. Salty tears ran down his cheeks, and his stomach hurt. He didn't know what to do. Grandmother was waiting for him on the front porch.

"What's wrong, Biyen?" said Peter's grandmother. Biyen was Peter's Ojibwe name. He called his grandmother Nokomis.

Peter looked up. "I have to give a presentation where I talk about a family **tradition**. I know we have lots of beliefs and customs. Can you **remind** me of one?"

Nokomis smiled and nodded her head.

"Come with me," she said.

FIND TEXT EVIDENCE

Read

Paragraphs 1–2
Plot: Character Development
How is Peter feeling when he gets home from school?

_____

_____

Circle text evidence that supports your answer.

Paragraphs 3–5
Character Perspective
Underline why Peter is upset. What does he ask Nokomis?

_____

_____

Reread

Author's Craft

How does the author help you understand about Peter's culture?

FIND TEXT EVIDENCE

Read

Paragraphs 1–3
Visualize
Underline details that help you picture what the dream catcher looks like.

Paragraph 4
Plot: Character Development
How have Peter's feelings changed from the beginning of the story? **Circle** text evidence.

_____

_____

_____

Why have Peter's feelings changed?

_____

_____

_____

Peter followed Nokomis. She went to a closet and stretched to reach the top shelf. She pulled out a small box and blew away the dust. She handed it to Peter.

"Open it," she said.

Peter opened the box. He spotted a wooden hoop inside. It was in the shape of a circle. String was woven and twisted around the hoop. It looked like a spider web. A black bead sat near the center. Feathers hung from the bottom.

Peter wiped away his tears and smiled.

"This is a dream catcher," said Nokomis. "Our people have made these for many generations. Circles are **symbols** of strength. Let's hang it over your bed tonight. It will catch your bad dreams in the web, and your good dreams will fall through the center. Maybe it will give you **courage** to do your presentation."

"Can I take this one to school?" asked Peter.

"No, Biyen," said Nokomis. "This dream catcher is **precious**. I got it when I was your age, and it means a lot to me."

FIND TEXT EVIDENCE

Read

Paragraph 1

Character Perspective

Underline what Nokomis says about the circles. How does Nokomis think the dream catcher will help Peter?

_____

_____

Paragraphs 2–3

Make Inferences

Why doesn't Nokomis want Peter to take her dream catcher to school?

_____

_____

Circle text evidence.

Reread

Author's Craft

How does the author help you understand that dream catchers are a tradition in Peter's family?

FIND TEXT EVIDENCE

Read

Paragraphs 1–3

Character Perspective

Draw a box around what Nokomis tells Peter they could do. How does Peter respond?

_____

_____

Paragraphs 4-5

Context Clues

Circle the word that helps you figure out what *gazed* means.

Plot: Character Development

What is Peter's plan?

_____

_____

Underline text evidence.

Reread

Author's Craft

How does the illustration help you understand how Peter feels about the dream catcher?

Peter felt **disappointment** because he wanted to share the dream catcher with his class.

"We could make you one," said Nokomis.

"I'd like that!" cried Peter.

Nokomis and Peter worked together and made a dream catcher. That night, as he gazed and looked at the dream catcher over his bed, he made a plan.

The next morning he told Nokomis his plan. "I'm going to show my class how to make a dream catcher," he said.

"That's a great idea!" said Nokomis. "Let's **celebrate** after your presentation. I will bake corn cookies and we will have a traditional Ojibwe party."

Peter shared his dream catcher with his classmates and showed them how to make their own. Peter didn't feel nervous or scared at all. He felt **pride** in his culture. He felt pride in himself, too.

Summarize

Use your notes and think about how Peter develops in "The Dream Catcher." Summarize the text using the story events.

FIND TEXT EVIDENCE

Read

Paragraph 1

Character Perspective

What does Nokomis think of Peter's plan? **Underline** what she says to Peter.

Visualize

Write something Nokomis and Peter will do at their party.

_____

_____

Paragraph 2

Plot: Character Development

How does Peter feel at the end of the story?

_____

_____

Circle text evidence.

Reread

Author's Craft

How does the author show how Peter changes during the story?

Vocabulary

Use the sentences to talk with a partner about each word. Then answer the questions.

celebrate

Kayla and her friends like to **celebrate** the Fourth of July together.

What do you like to celebrate?

_____

_____

courage

Firefighters show bravery and **courage**.

What word means the same as *courage*?

_____

_____

Build Your Word List Pick one of the interesting words you wrote down on page 40. Use a thesaurus to look up the word. Write the word and two of its synonyms and antonyms in your reader's notebook.

disappointment

Jason felt **disappointment** when his class trip was canceled.

What would make you feel disappointment?

_____

_____

precious

This necklace is **precious** to my grandmother because her mother gave it to her.

Name something that is precious to you.

_____

_____

pride

I take **pride** in my drawings.

When do you feel pride?

_____

_____

remind

Mom will **remind** me to clean my room.

What is something someone needs to remind you to do?

_____

_____

symbols

The eagle and the flag are **symbols** of our country.

Name another symbol.

_____

_____

tradition

My family's Thanksgiving **tradition** is to cook dinner together.

Describe a tradition people share.

_____

_____

Context Clues

If you come across a word you don't know, use context clues. Look for other words in the same sentence that can help you figure out the unfamiliar word's meaning.

🔍 **FIND TEXT EVIDENCE**

I read this sentence on page 41. I'm not sure what the word presentation _means. I see the words_ talk about. _This clue helps me figure out what_ presentation _means. A presentation is a talk or speech._

I have to give a presentation where I talk about a family tradition.

Your Turn Use context clues to figure out the meaning of the word.

woven, page 42 _____

_____

CHECK IN 1 2 3 4

Visualize

As you read, use details to visualize, or form pictures in your mind. This will help you better understand the text.

🔍 FIND TEXT EVIDENCE

Where does Nokomis keep her dream catcher? Use the details in the first paragraph on page 42.

Quick Tip

To help you visualize, pay attention to verbs, or words that show action, to understand what a person or thing does. Adjectives, or words that describe nouns, can also help you visualize.

Page 42

Peter followed Nokomis. She went to a closet and stretched to reach the top shelf. She pulled out a small box and blew away the dust. She handed it to Peter.

"Open it," she said.

I can visualize where Nokomis keeps her dream catcher. It's on the top shelf of the closet, in a small box covered in dust. These details show the dream catcher has been in a safe space for a long time.

Your Turn Reread the first paragraph on page 43. Talk with your partner about what you visualize. What does Nokomis's description of the dream catcher help you understand?

_____

_____

_____

CHECK IN ▸ 1 ▸ 2 ▸ 3 ▸ 4

Character Perspective

"The Dream Catcher" is **realistic fiction**. Realistic fiction

- has a made-up story with a beginning, middle, and end
- has a plot, or story events, that could really happen
- usually has dialogue that can show the perspectives, or thoughts and feelings, of different characters

 **FIND TEXT EVIDENCE**

"The Dream Catcher" is realistic fiction. The story events could really happen. Characters share their thoughts through dialogue.

Page 41

Peter walked home from school. Salty tears ran down his cheeks, and his stomach hurt. He didn't know what to do. Grandmother was waiting for him on the front porch.

"What's wrong, Biyen?" said Peter's grandmother. Biyen was Peter's Ojibwe name. He called his grandmother Nokomis.

Peter looked up. "I have to give a presentation where I talk about a family **tradition**. I know we have lots of beliefs and customs. Can you **remind** me of one?"

Nokomis smiled and nodded her head.

"Come with me," she said.

Readers to Writers

Reread the dialogue in "The Dream Catcher." What does it tell you about the characters? Use dialogue in your own writing to show what your characters think and feel about other characters and situations.

Character Perspective

A character's perspective is what he or she thinks or feels about something. Characters often reveal their perspectives through dialogue, or what they say.

 **Your Turn** Reread page 43. How does Nokomis's dialogue help you understand why her dream catcher is important?

_____

_____

_____

CHECK IN 1 > 2 > 3 > 4 >

Plot: Character Development

Characters in fiction develop, or change, throughout a story's plot. To understand how characters develop, look for changes in their feelings and actions in the beginning, middle, and end of a story.

 FIND TEXT EVIDENCE

The beginning of the story describes how Peter feels and shows how he responds to needing to give a presentation. I read on to see how his feelings and actions change in the middle and end.

Character
Peter

Setting
Nokomis's house

Beginning
Peter is crying, and his stomach hurts. He doesn't know what to do about his presentation.

Middle

End

 **Your Turn** Reread pages 42–45. How do Peter's feelings and actions change in the middle and end? List them in your graphic organizer.

CHECK IN 1 2 3 4

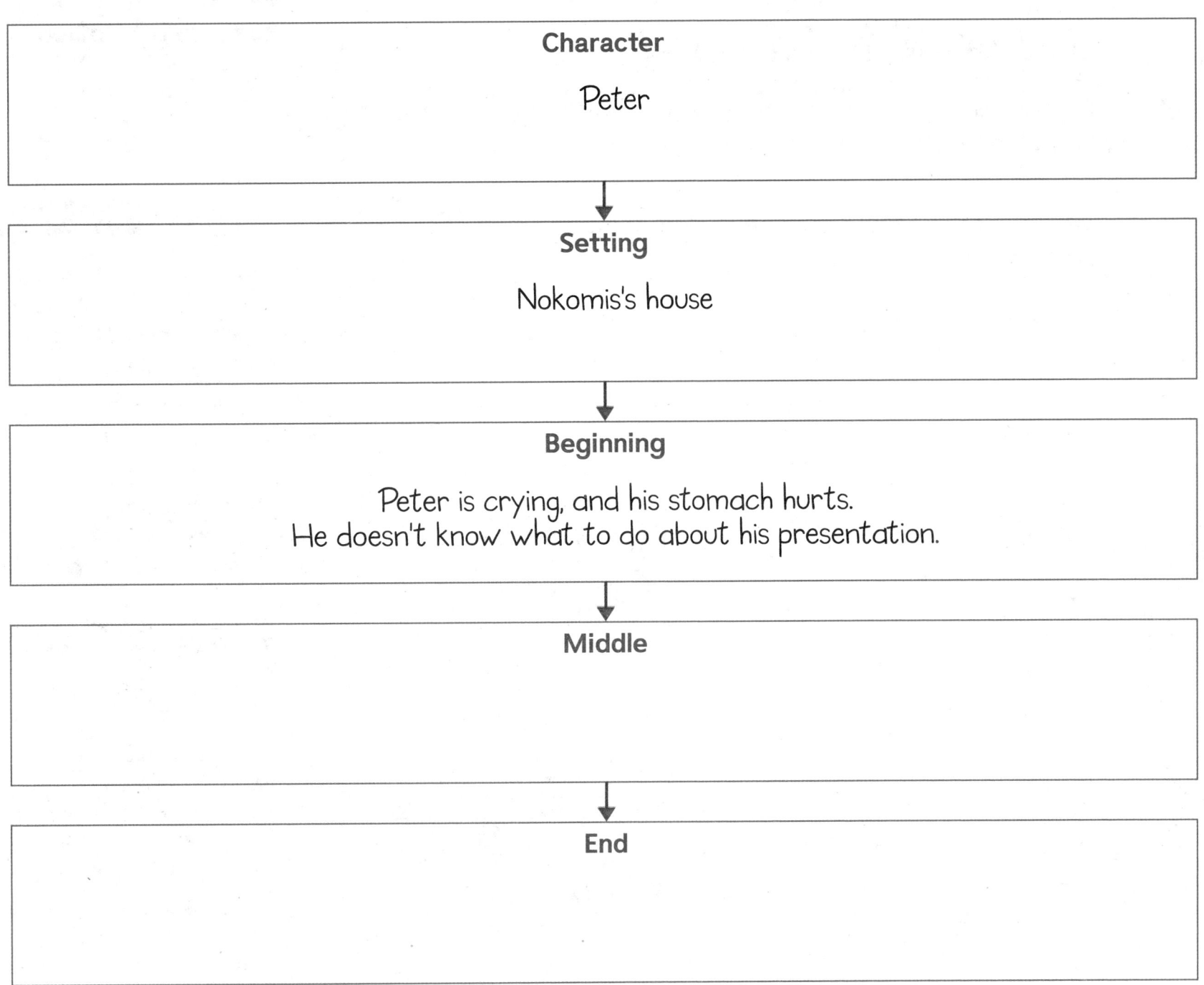

Character

Peter

Setting

Nokomis's house

Beginning

Peter is crying, and his stomach hurts.
He doesn't know what to do about his presentation.

Middle

End

I can use text evidence to respond to realistic fiction.

Respond to Reading

COLLABORATE

Talk about the prompt below. Use your notes and evidence from the text to support your answer.

Why do Peter's feelings change from the beginning of the story to the end?

_____

_____

_____

_____

_____

_____

_____

Quick Tip

Use these sentence starters to talk about how Peter feels.

At the beginning, I read that Peter . . .

At the end of the story, Peter . . .

The reason for this change is . . .

Grammar Connections

After you write your response, read it over to make sure you're using complete sentences. This helps you make sure your response makes sense.

CHECK IN 1 > 2 > 3 > 4

Cultural Traditions

COLLABORATE

A culture quilt is a great way to learn about cultural traditions. Work with a partner to brainstorm a list of family or community traditions you practice. Then follow the research process to make a square for a class culture quilt.

Step 1 Set a Goal Choose a tradition from your list. Think of questions about it that you can answer through research.

Step 2 Identify Sources Use formal inquiry by finding books, encyclopedias, and reliable websites that answer your questions. Use informal inquiry by finding family members or others who know about your tradition.

Step 3 Find and Record Information Gather information from your sources that answers your questions. Cite your sources.

Step 4 Organize and Combine Information Use your information to write a paragraph about your tradition on a square of paper.

Step 5 Create and Present Draw a picture of the tradition on the other side of the square. Think about how you will present what you've learned to the class.

> **Quick Tip**
>
> Questions you may ask about your tradition include: When is this tradition practiced? How is it practiced? What is its history?

Sean Justice/Fuse/ Getty Images

CHECK IN 1 > 2 > 3 > 4

Yoon and the Jade Bracelet

How does the author help you understand how Yoon feels about the present her mother gives her?

Literature Anthology: pages 26–43

Talk About It Reread **Literature Anthology** page 28. Talk with a partner about the present Yoon really wants for her birthday. How do you know?

Cite Text Evidence What words and phrases show how Yoon feels? Write text evidence here.

 Make Inferences

An inference is a conclusion based on evidence. What inference can you make about why Yoon smiles even though she is disappointed?

Text Evidence	How Yoon Feels

Write The author helps me understand how Yoon feels about the

present by _____

_____

_____

CHECK IN 1 2 3 4

How do you know jade is important in Yoon's culture?

Talk About It Reread the last paragraph on **Literature Anthology** page 31. Talk about what Yoon's mother says about jade.

Cite Text Evidence What clues help you see that jade is important in Yoon's culture? Write text evidence in the chart.

Yoon's Mother Says	This Tells Me

Write I know that jade is important to Yoon's culture because

_____

_____

_____

Quick Tip

I can use these sentence starters to talk about jade.

Yoon's mother uses words such as . . .

This helps me understand that jade is . . .

 Evaluate Information

Think about the different things Yoon's mother says about jade. What do these different things have in common?

CHECK IN 1 2 3 4

? **How does the author show that the children in Yoon's class are her friends?**

Talk About It Reread **Literature Anthology** page 39. Talk with a partner about what Yoon's classmates do and say.

Cite Text Evidence What do Yoon's classmates do and say when their teacher asks about the bracelet? Write clues in the chart.

 Make Inferences

An inference is a conclusion based on facts. Use what you know to make an inference about how Yoon's classmates feel about her.

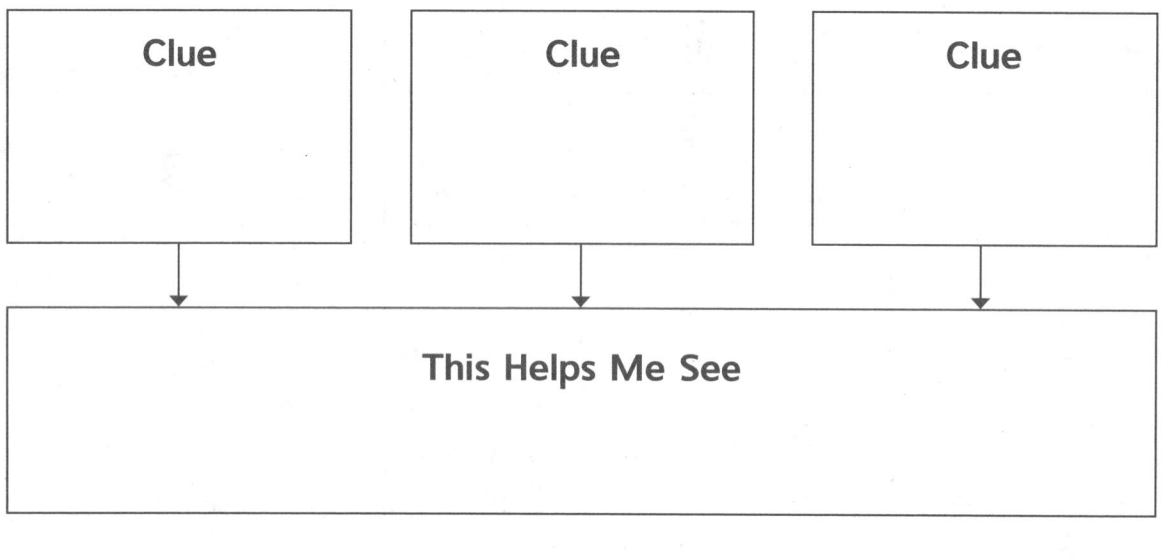

| Clue | Clue | Clue |

This Helps Me See

Write I know the children are Yoon's friends because the author

_____

_____

_____

CHECK IN 1 2 3 4

Respond to Reading

COLLABORATE

Talk about the prompt below. Use your notes and evidence from the text to support your answer.

How do you know that Yoon's Korean name, Shining Wisdom, is a good name for her?

Quick Tip

Use these sentence starters to talk about Yoon's name.

Shining Wisdom is a good name for Yoon because . . .

Yoon shows she is wise by . . .

Literature Anthology: pages 46–49

Family Traditions

Celebrating a New Year

1   Chinese families celebrate Lunar New Year. Lunar New Year happens in January or February. It lasts about two weeks. The holiday means that winter is ending. Spring is on the way!

2   The traditions for Lunar New Year are very old. Adults give children bright red envelopes. Red stands for good luck and happiness. The envelopes are full of good luck money.

3   This holiday is also a time for feasts. Chinese families share sweet, smooth rice cakes. Some families eat a whole cooked fish. They give oranges as presents. They eat noodles, too. These foods are symbols for a happy year and long life.

4   In most big cities, families watch the Lunar New Year parade. Dragon dancers glide down the street. Lion dancers wear costumes in red, yellow, and green. Bands march by in rows. Their drums beat out happy tunes. People in traditional costumes go by on floats. They wave to the crowd. BANG! Watch out for firecrackers! They are part of the tradition, too. Loud sounds are symbols of a joyful time of year.

Reread and use the prompts to take notes in the text.

Reread paragraph 1. **Draw a star** before the sentence that explains what the Lunar New Year means. Write it here.

_____

_____

Now reread paragraphs 2–4. **Underline** Lunar New Year traditions.

COLLABORATE

Talk with a partner about Lunar New Year traditions. **Circle** words the author uses to help you picture things you might see at a Lunar New Year feast and parade.

Storytelling and Dance

1   Many Native American cultures have traditions of storytelling and dance. The stories are from long ago. Older people tell the stories to their children and grandchildren. They may use the culture's native language. The stories explain things in nature. They tell about the courage of early people.

2   Some Native American groups get together in the summer. They meet at big powwows. These festivals celebrate culture through dance and music. Storytellers bring the old tales to life. The soft notes of a flute may help tell a story. The firm beat of a drum adds power. People from other cultures can watch and listen. Everyone enjoys the stories and learns about the traditions.

Reread paragraph 1. **Circle** two Native American traditions. Which tradition does the paragraph describe?

_____

Underline two things the Native American stories are about.

COLLABORATE

With a partner, reread paragraph 2. Talk about how the author describes powwows. **Draw a box around** the things you might hear at a powwow.

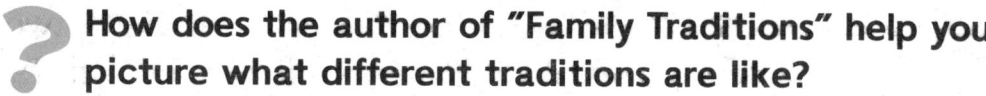

How does the author of "Family Traditions" help you picture what different traditions are like?

Talk About It Look back at your notes. Talk with a partner about what you've learned about different traditions.

Cite Text Evidence What words does the author use to help you picture the ways families share traditions? Write them in the web.

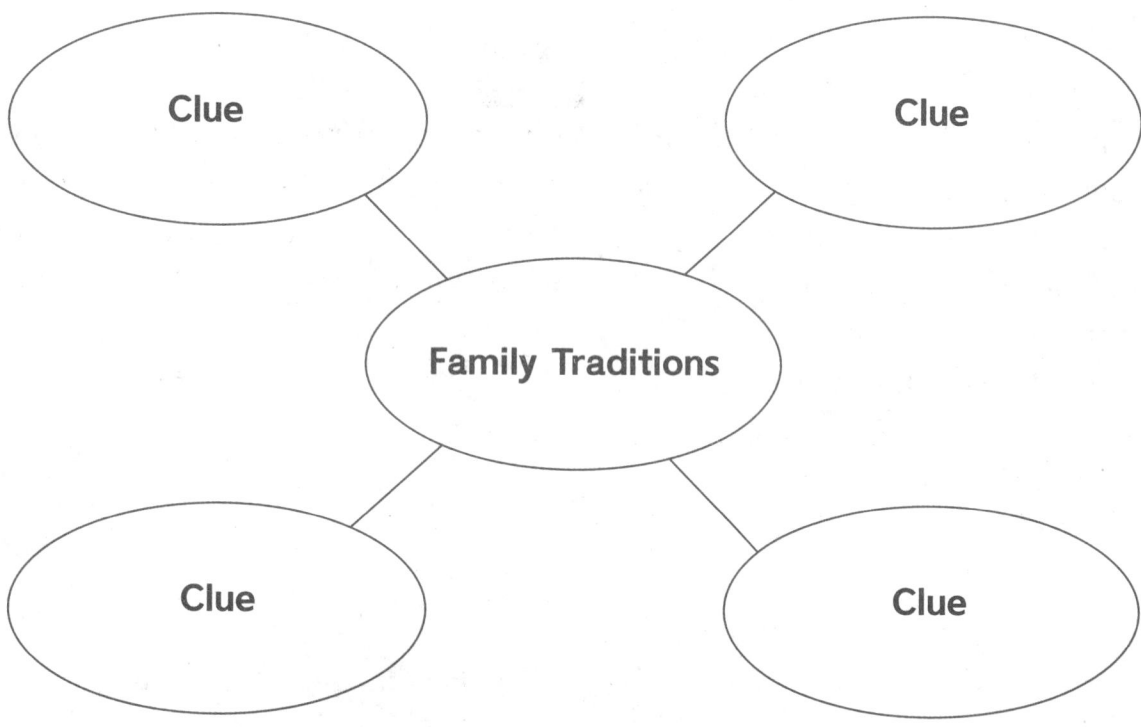

Clue

Clue

Family Traditions

Clue

Clue

Write The author helps me picture what traditions are like by

_____

_____

CHECK IN 1 > 2 > 3 > 4

Author's Purpose

In an expository text, the author's purpose is to inform the reader about a topic. Authors do this by using interesting and descriptive words and phrases that help readers understand unfamiliar ideas.

FIND TEXT EVIDENCE

On page 47 of the **Literature Anthology**, the author of "Family Traditions" uses words and phrases such as "drums beat out happy tunes" and "BANG!" This helps the author show how the celebrations are full of fun and excitement.

> Bands march by in rows. Their drums beat out happy tunes. People in traditional costumes go by on floats. They wave to the crowd. BANG! Watch out for firecrackers!

Your Turn Reread the last paragraph on page 49.

- What phrases does the author use to describe traditions?

_____

- What do these phrases help you understand about traditions?

_____

CHECK IN 1 2 3 4

? **How is the family in the photograph like the families in *Yoon and the Jade Bracelet* and "Family Traditions"?**

Talk About It With a partner, talk about what the family in the photograph is doing. Choose one clue that shows a tradition, and talk about how you know it's important.

Cite Text Evidence Look at the photograph. Think about what is special to Yoon's mother and how the families in "Family Traditions" celebrate special days. **Circle** clues that show that the dinner is special. Then read the caption. **Draw a box around** text that helps you know this is a family tradition.

Write The families in the photograph and

selections are similar because _____

_____

_____

_____

_____

This family lives in Richmond, Virginia. They celebrate every Thanksgiving at their grandmother's house.

CHECK IN 1 2 3 4

My Goal I know how traditions can teach us about cultures.

Make an Invitation

Think over the texts you read that tell how traditions teach us about different cultures. Why do you think it's important to learn about cultural traditions? Use text evidence to support your ideas.

1. Look at your Build Knowledge notes in your reader's notebook.

2. Create an invitation to a festival that celebrates the different cultures in your community. Describe the events and activities someone might see at the festival. Explain why learning about different cultural traditions is important. Use new vocabulary words you have learned.

3. Include the time, place, and location of the festival on your invitation. Add drawings of what people might see.

Think about what you learned in this text set. Fill in the bars on page 39.

Build Knowledge

How do landmarks help us understand our country's story?

Build Vocabulary

Write new words you learned about landmarks and monuments. Draw lines and circles for the words you write.

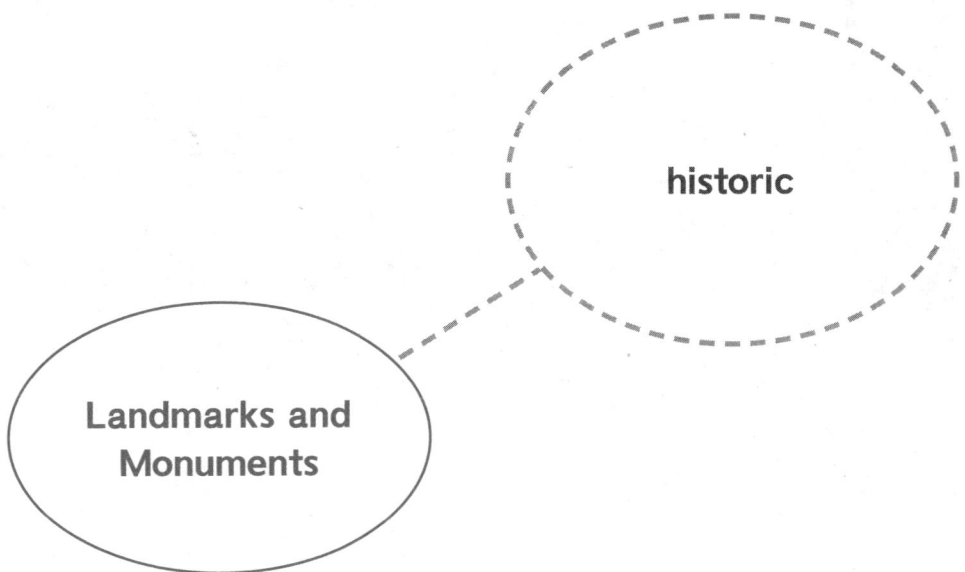

historic

Landmarks and Monuments

Go online to **my.mheducation.com** and read the "Special Places" Blast. Think about why learning about landmarks is important. Then blast back your response.

Think about what you already know. Fill in the bars. You'll keep learning more.

What I Know Now

I can read and understand argumentative text.

| 1 | 2 | 3 | 4 |

I can use text evidence to respond to argumentative text.

| 1 | 2 | 3 | 4 |

I know how landmarks help us understand our country's story.

| 1 | 2 | 3 | 4 |

Key

1 =	I do not understand.
2 =	I understand but need more practice.
3 =	I understand.
4 =	I understand and can teach someone.

STOP You will come back to the next page later.

What I Learned

I can read and understand argumentative text.

1 > 2 > 3 > 4

I can use text evidence to respond to argumentative text.

1 > 2 > 3 > 4

I know how landmarks help us understand our country's story.

1 > 2 > 3 > 4

Think about what you learned. Fill in the bars. Keep up the good work!

My Goal I can read and understand argumentative text.

TAKE NOTES

As you read, make note of interesting words and important information.

_____

_____

_____

_____

_____

_____

_____

_____

TIME **KiDS**

Preserve and Protect

Essential Question

?

How do landmarks help us understand our country's story?

Read about why national parks are important.

The largest living tree in the world lives in a forest in California. But not just any forest. This **massive** tree lives in the Giant Forest. It is a **landmark** that has been growing there for over 2,000 years. Many people work hard to protect this **national** treasure. There are rules to make sure this happens. But some people worry that there are too many rules.

A GIANT FOREST

More than one million people hike the trails in the Giant Forest to visit the General Sherman Tree each year. It's no wonder. The **grand** sequoia tree stands 275 feet tall. It is almost as wide as a school bus is long. But many other huge trees live there, too. The Giant Forest is where half of the Earth's sequoia trees live.

In 1964, President Lyndon B. Johnson signed a law that protects trees like the General Sherman. It also protects all plants and animals living in national parks. The law states that animals and wildlife are safe there. No one can cut trees or build homes on the land. The **traces**, or parts, of cultures that lived there long ago are protected. National parks protect thousands and thousands of acres of wildlife. But some people believe these lands should be available for other uses.

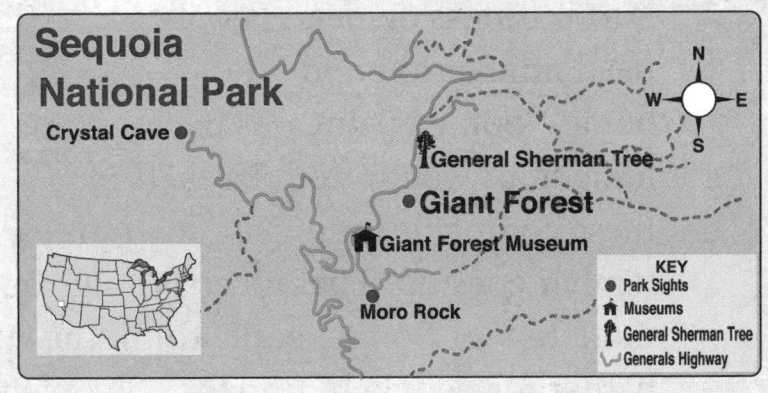

Sequoia National Park

Crystal Cave ●

General Sherman Tree

● Giant Forest

Giant Forest Museum

Moro Rock

N W E S

KEY
- ● Park Sights
- Museums
- General Sherman Tree
- Generals Highway

The Sequoia National Park is located in California.

ARGUMENTATIVE TEXT

FIND TEXT EVIDENCE

Read

Paragraph 1

Ask and Answer Questions
What are some people worried about? **Underline** text evidence. Now think of a question you might have. Write it here.

_____

_____

Paragraphs 2–3

Central Idea and Details
Circle three details that tell about the Giant Forest.

Maps

Look at the map key. **Draw a box around** the General Sherman tree. Write the name of another place from the map.

_____

Reread

Author's Craft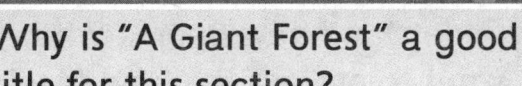

Why is "A Giant Forest" a good title for this section?

FIND TEXT EVIDENCE

Read

Paragraph 1

Central Idea and Details

Underline three details that tell what the rules protect.

Paragraph 2

Multiple-Meaning Words

Draw a box around clues that help you figure out what *past* means. Write what it means.

Paragraph 3

Ask and Answer Questions

Ask a question about the lumber business. Write it here.

Reread

Author's Craft

How does the author help you understand how people who want to protect the land feel?

Protect the Land!

Millions of people visit national parks each year. Nature lovers hike the trails. They explore caves **carved** out of mountains. They admire hundreds of different plants and animals. These people agree with President Johnson. They like the rules that protect the land. They believe the rules help keep our country's forests and animals safe. They think all people should visit and enjoy them. They think people can learn from nature.

Visiting a national **monument** is a way to learn about history. Monuments preserve traces of past cultures so that they don't get destroyed. Scientists rely on these **clues** to help them learn about how people lived long ago.

What About My Business?

Other people think there are too many rules that protect the land. They believe those rules hurt business owners. People need lumber to build new homes. Some businesses make lumber, or wood, from trees. If

Lumber businesses rely on trees to make money.

these companies can't cut down trees, the price of lumber goes up. That means things built with wood cost more to buy. Some people think the rules also make it harder for people to find jobs. People who cut down trees or build new houses have to find new jobs.

abodonian/iStock/Getty Images

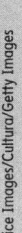
Juice Images/Cultura/Getty Images

To Protect or Not to Protect?

Today the United States has hundreds of national parks, monuments, and landmarks. Animals and plants live in them. Visitors enjoy them. Scientists learn from them. The rules protect them. But are there too many rules? Not everyone agrees.

Is It a Park or a Monument?

A United States national monument is a protected area. It is like a national park, but easier to create. Monuments and parks are different in other important ways.

National Monuments

- often focus on protecting one specific natural resource, landmark, or structure that has historic or scientific interest
- receive less money and less wildlife protection than parks

National Parks

- are large natural places with many different natural features
- aim to protect many different aspects of nature

Summarize

Review the notes you took on "Preserve and Protect." Summarize the text using the central idea and details.

FIND TEXT EVIDENCE

Read

Paragraph 1

Multiple-Meaning Words

Find the word *parks*. **Circle** clues that help you figure out its meaning. Write what it means.

Sidebar

Central Idea and Details

Underline details that tell what a national monument is.

Sidebars

What information does the sidebar give you? **Draw a box around** text evidence.

Reread

Author's Craft

How does the sidebar help you understand how monuments and parks are different?

Vocabulary

Use the sentences to talk with a partner about each word. Then answer the questions.

carved

An artist **carved** the statue out of rock.

What other things can be carved?

_____

_____

clues

Paw prints are **clues** that an animal walked by recently.

What clues tell you that it might rain?

_____

_____

grand

The family sat and gazed at the **grand** view of the river.

What else would make a grand view?

_____

_____

landmark

The Statue of Liberty is an American **landmark**.

What other landmarks can you name?

_____

_____

massive

The boaters looked up at the **massive** cliff.

What is another word for *massive*?

_____

_____

Build Your Word List Pick one of the interesting words you listed on page 68. Use a print or online dictionary to find the word's meaning. Then use the word in a sentence in your reader's notebook.

monument

A **monument** that honors Martin Luther King Jr. stands in Washington, DC.

Describe a monument you have seen.

_____

_____

national

The Fourth of July is a **national** holiday.

Name another national holiday.

_____

_____

traces

In the morning, we found **traces**, or small amounts, of snow on the plants.

What does *traces* mean?

_____

_____

Multiple-Meaning Words

Multiple-meaning words have more than one meaning. Find other words in the sentence, or beyond the sentence, to help you figure out the meaning of a multiple-meaning word.

FIND TEXT EVIDENCE

On page 69, I see the word feet. *This word can mean "the body part humans walk on" or "a measure of length." The context clues* stands *and* tall *help me figure out that here* feet *refers to the length of something.*

The grand sequoia tree stands 275 feet tall.

Your Turn Use context clues to figure out the meanings of the following words.

plants, page 70 _____

safe, page 70 _____

CHECK IN 1 2 3 4

P. Burghardt/Shutterstock

Ask and Answer Questions

Ask yourself questions as you read. Look for details to support your answers. This will help you better understand a text.

 **FIND TEXT EVIDENCE**

Reread the section "Protect the Land!" on page 70. Think of a question. Then reread to answer it.

> Page 70
>
> TIME **KiDS** **Protect the Land!**
>
> Millions of people visit national parks each year. Nature lovers hike the trails. They explore caves **carved** out of mountains. They admire hundreds of different plants and animals. These people agree with President Johnson. They like the rules that protect the land. They believe the rules help keep our country's forests and animals safe. They think all people should visit and enjoy them. They think people can learn from nature.
>
> Visiting a national **monument** is a way to learn about history. Monuments preserve traces of past cultures so that they don't get destroyed. Scientists rely on these **clues** to help them learn about how people lived long ago.

I have a question. What do people do when they visit national parks? I read that people hike the trails. They explore caves. They admire the plants and animals. Now I can answer my question. People visit national parks for many reasons.

 **Your Turn** Reread the last paragraph on page 70. Think of one question. You might ask, *How do the rules hurt business owners?* Write your question below. Read the section again to find the answer. Then write the answer next to your question.

CHECK IN 〉 1 〉 2 〉 3 〉 4 〉

Captions, Maps, and Sidebars

"Preserve and Protect" is an **argumentative text**. Argumentative text
- is nonfiction stating the author's claim on a topic
- gives facts and examples to persuade the reader to agree with the author's claim, or statement that something is true
- may include text features, such as captions, maps, and sidebars

FIND TEXT EVIDENCE

I can tell that "Preserve and Protect" is an argumentative text. It has points for and counterpoints against protecting wild land. It includes facts about why the land should be protected and why it should be used as a resource by businesses.

Page 71

To Protect or Not to Protect?

Today the United States has hundreds of national parks, monuments, and landmarks. Animals and plants live in them. Visitors enjoy them. Scientists learn from them. The rules protect them. But are there too many rules? Not everyone agrees.

Is It a Park or a Monument?

A United States national monument is a protected area. It is like a national park, but easier to create. Monuments and parks are different in other important ways.

National Parks
- are large natural places with many different natural features
- aim to protect many different aspects of nature

National Monuments
- often focus on protecting one specific natural resource, landmark, or structure that has historic or scientific interest
- receive less money and less wildlife protection than parks

Summarize

Review the notes you took on "Preserve and Protect." Summarize the text using the central idea and details.

Captions

Captions give information that is not in the main text.

Sidebars

A sidebar gives more information related to the topic.

COLLABORATE

Your Turn Find more text features in "Preserve and Protect." What else did you learn? Write your answer below.

_____

_____

_____

CHECK IN 1 > 2 > 3 > 4

Central Idea and Relevant Details

The central, or main, idea is the most important point an author makes about a topic. Relevant details tell more information about the topic and support the central idea.

🔍 FIND TEXT EVIDENCE

"Protect the Land!" on page 70 is about why rules that protect parks are good. I can look for details related to this topic. Then I'll see what the details have in common to find the central idea.

Central Idea
Many people agree with rules that protect national parks.
Detail
They believe rules keep our forests and animals safe.
Detail
They think rules preserve traces of past cultures that teach us about history.

 **Your Turn** Reread "What About My Business?" on page 70. Add relevant details to the graphic organizer. Use the details to find the central idea. Explain why they support the central idea.

CHECK IN ⟩ 1 ⟩ 2 ⟩ 3 ⟩ 4

Central Idea

Detail

Detail

Detail

Respond to Reading

COLLABORATE Talk about the prompt below. Use your notes and evidence from the text to support your answer.

Do you think it's more important to protect the land or let businesses cut down trees? Use text evidence to support your claim.

_____

_____

_____

_____

_____

_____

_____

_____

_____

Quick Tip

Use these sentence starters to talk about your opinion, or claim.

I think it's more important to . . .

One reason for my opinion is . . .

Grammar Connections

As you write, use a variety of sentences, including simple and compound sentences. Use the correct punctuation and conjunction in each compound sentence.

CHECK IN 1 2 3 4

 SOCIAL STUDIES

Landmarks in Your State

Postcards that people send their friends and family often show important landmarks. Follow the research process to create a postcard for a landmark in your state. Work with a partner.

Step 1 **Set a Goal** Brainstorm a list of landmarks in your state. They can be natural or made by people. Choose one landmark to include on your postcard.

Step 2 **Identify Sources** Use books and reliable websites to find information about your landmark.

Step 3 **Find and Record Information** Use your sources to find facts about your landmark. Take notes and remember to cite your sources.

Step 4 **Organize and Combine Information** Choose the three most interesting facts you found about your landmark. Think about how the facts can be used to convince people to visit it.

Step 5 **Create and Present** Create your final postcard. Draw a picture of your landmark on one side. On the other, write why people should visit it. Include facts to support your opinion. Say what the landmark can teach people about your state.

Quick Tip

Facts are statements that can be proven true. Opinions are statements based on feelings. Writers use facts to support their opinions and convince readers to agree with them.

Greetings from CALIFORNIA

The General Sherman tree is very old. It is 275 feet tall. This tree is amazing, and you should go see it!

(t)mhgstan/Shutterstock, (b)Filipe Frazao/Shutterstock

CHECK IN 1 2 3 4

Protecting Our Parks

Literature Anthology:
pages 50–53

? How does the author help you understand why the National Park System is important?

Talk About It Reread **Literature Anthology** page 51. Talk with a partner about what the National Park System does.

Cite Text Evidence What facts does the author use to show that the National Park System is important? Write them here.

Combine Information

Use what you know about protecting wildlife and the facts the author gives to help you understand why the National Park System is important.

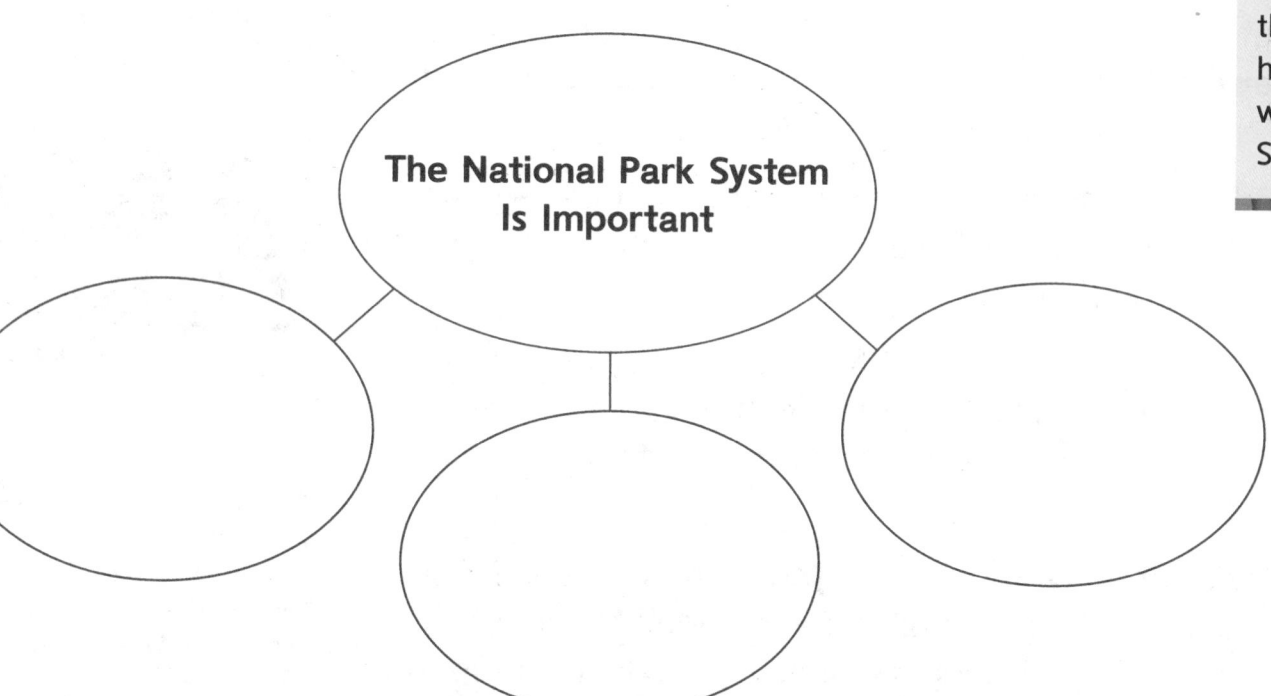

The National Park System Is Important

Write I understand why the National Park System is important

because the author _____

_____

CHECK IN 1 2 3 4

? How does the author help you understand the different claims people make about park visitors?

Talk About It Reread **Literature Anthology** pages 52 and 53. Talk with a partner about the claims expressed in "Allow All Access" and "Protect Our Parks."

Cite Text Evidence What facts and details support each claim? Write them in the chart.

Allow All Access	Protect Our Parks

Write I understand the different claims people make about park visitors because the author _____

_____

_____

_____

_____

Quick Tip

When you read an argumentative text, think about who the intended audience or reader might be. Ask yourself, "Who is the author trying to convince or persuade?"

 Make Inferences

By using evidence from the text and your own experience with other argumentative texts, make an inference about who the intended audience, or reader, is for "Protecting Our Parks."

CHECK IN 1 > 2 > 3 > 4

Respond to Reading

My Goal I can use text evidence to respond to argumentative text.

Talk about the prompt below. Use your notes and evidence from the text to support your answer.

COLLABORATE

What would you do to protect our parks? Use text evidence to support your choice.

_____

_____

_____

_____

_____

_____

_____

_____

_____

_____

Quick Tip

Use these sentence starters to talk about protecting our parks.

One thing I would do to protect our parks is . . .

Another thing that could help is . . .

CHECK IN 1 > 2 > 3 > 4

5 Questions for George McDonald

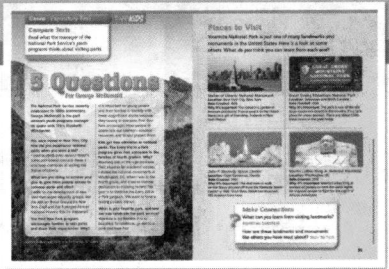

Literature Anthology: pages 54–55

The National Park Service recently celebrated its 100th anniversary. George McDonald is the park service's youth programs manager. He spoke with TFK's Elizabeth Winchester.

The Find Your Park program encourages families to visit parks and share their experiences. Why?
It is important for young people and their families to identify with these magnificent places because they belong to everyone. Find Your Park encourages more people to appreciate our country's valuable resources, and to also protect them.

The Every Kid in a Park program gives free admission to the families of fourth graders. Why?
Reaching kids at this age increases their chances for academic success.

Reread and use the prompts to take notes in the text.

Reread the first two questions and answers. **Circle** the names of national park programs that are important to George McDonald. Write them here.

_____

_____

COLLABORATE

Reread the introduction with a partner. **Underline** details that tell you more about George McDonald and his connection to national parks. Talk about why the author chose him to answer questions about national parks.

? **How do you know what the Find Your Park and Every Kid in a Park programs do?**

 **Talk About It** Reread the excerpt on page 83. Talk with a partner about the Find Your Park and Every Kid in a Park programs.

Cite Text Evidence How does the interview help you understand what the Find Your Park and Every Kid in a Park programs do? Write text evidence in the chart.

Find Your Park	Every Kid in a Park

Write I know what the Find Your Park and Every Kid in a Park

programs do because _____

_____

_____

_____

_____

CHECK IN 1 2 3 4

Author's Claim

A claim is a statement that something is true. In opinion writing, authors support their claims with reasons and evidence, such as facts and examples.

 **FIND TEXT EVIDENCE**

On page 83, George McDonald makes a claim about the importance of visiting national parks. *It is important for young people and their families to identify with these magnificent places.* He supports this by saying parks belong to everyone.

> It is important for young people and their families to identify with these magnificent places because they belong to everyone.

Your Turn Reread page 54 in the **Literature Anthology**. What is another claim George McDonald makes?

_____

_____

How does George McDonald support this claim?

_____

_____

Readers to Writers

Think about how you can convince readers to agree with your own claims. What evidence is most likely to convince the reader to agree with you?

CHECK IN 1 > 2 > 3 > 4 >

? **How is the message of the illustration below like the message of "Protecting Our Parks" and "5 Questions for George McDonald"?**

COLLABORATE

Talk About It With a partner, talk about what you see in the illustration. Choose some of the things you see, and discuss why people would want to visit this place.

Cite Text Evidence Circle two things in the illustration you talked about with your partner. Read the caption. **Underline** clues in the caption that inform people about America.

Write The messages of F. F. Palmer's illustration and the texts I read this week are

alike because _____

_____

_____

_____

_____

_____

Quick Tip

I see clues in the painting that help tell America's story. This will help me compare text to art.

F. F. Palmer is known for her illustrations of American life. She created *The Mountain Pass* in 1867. It shows the Sierra Nevada mountain range, one of America's most beautiful landmarks and the center of the California Gold Rush, which began in 1848.

CHECK IN ⟩ 1 ⟩ 2 ⟩ 3 ⟩ 4 ⟩

 **My Goal** I know how landmarks help us understand our country's story.

Plan a Trip

Think about the texts you read that describe landmarks and monuments. Why is it important to protect our country's landmarks? Use text evidence to support your ideas.

1. Look at your Build Knowledge notes in your reader's notebook.

2. Plan a trip to help your friends learn more about the United States through its monuments and landmarks. Describe at least three places your friends should visit. Write what your friends can learn from visiting them. Tell why the landmarks and monuments are important to protect. Try to use new vocabulary words you learned in your writing.

3. Add some drawings to your plan to help your friends picture what they will see on their trip.

Think about what you learned in this text set. Fill in the bars on page 67.

Think about what you already know. Fill in the bars. Meeting your goals may take time.

Key

1 = I do not understand.

2 = I understand but need more practice.

3 = I understand.

4 = I understand and can teach someone.

What I Know Now

I can write a personal narrative.

| 1 | 2 | 3 | 4 |

I can write an opinion essay.

| 1 | 2 | 3 | 4 |

STOP You will come back to the next page later.

> Think about what you learned. Fill in the bars. What do you want to work on more?

What I Learned

I can write a personal narrative.

1 > 2 > 3 > 4

I can write an opinion essay.

1 > 2 > 3 > 4

Expert Model

Features of a Personal Narrative

A personal narrative is a kind of narrative nonfiction. A personal narrative

- tells about a true story of a person's life in order
- shares the writer's feelings about an experience
- has a beginning, middle, and end

Literature Anthology: pages 10–21

Analyze an Expert Model Reread the last paragraph on page 11 of *Gary the Dreamer* in the **Literature Anthology**. Use text evidence to answer the questions.

How does Gary Soto make reading about his pets more

interesting? _____

_____

_____

What does the last sentence tell you about Gary? _____

_____

_____

Word Wise

Writers use pronouns, such as *I, we, she, he, him,* and *her,* to take the place of nouns. For example, Gary Soto says, "Once, when Boots came by, I tossed a piece of bark at *him.*" The pronoun *him* stands for Boots. Pronouns can tell readers if authors are writing about themselves or someone else.

Plan: Choose Your Topic

COLLABORATE

Brainstorm With a partner, brainstorm memories of when you tried your hardest to do something. Use the sentence starters below to talk about your ideas.

I remember when . . .

This made me feel . . .

Writing Prompt Choose one of your memories to write about in a personal narrative.

I will write about _____

_____

_____

Purpose and Audience An author's purpose is the main reason for writing. Your audience is who will be reading it.

Who will read your personal narrative? _____

_____

_____

_____

Plan Think about what you want your readers to learn about you. Ask yourself questions and answer them in your writer's notebook.

Quick Tip

When you write a personal narrative, you are sharing your thoughts and feelings with your audience. As you plan your personal narrative, ask yourself: *What do I want people to remember about my narrative?*

CHECK IN 1 2 3 4

Plan: Sequence of Events

Quick Tip

Every narrative needs a beginning, middle, and end. Transitional words and phrases that show time order can help readers keep track of the sequence of events. For example, *finally*, *at last*, or *in the end* help readers know they are reaching the end of the narrative.

Sequence of Events Authors use a logical sequence of events to tell their narratives. Telling events in time order, or the order that they happened, makes your writing easier for readers to follow.

Let's look at another expert model. Read this passage from "Room to Grow."

> First she and Papa planted seeds in pots. Then they hung them from hooks. Next they crammed plants onto shelves. Green vines tumbled over desks. Soon our house had plants everywhere.

Authors use transitional words and phrases, such as *first*, *then*, and *finally*, to move from one event to the next. Reread the passage above and **circle** four transitional words.

 Think of the memory you will write about. Talk with a partner about what you did. Use these sentence starters to tell your story:

First, I . . .
Then, I . . .
Finally, I . . .

 **Chart** In your writer's notebook, draw a Sequence of Events chart. Complete the chart with the events that make up the beginning, middle, and end of your narrative. Use transitional words.

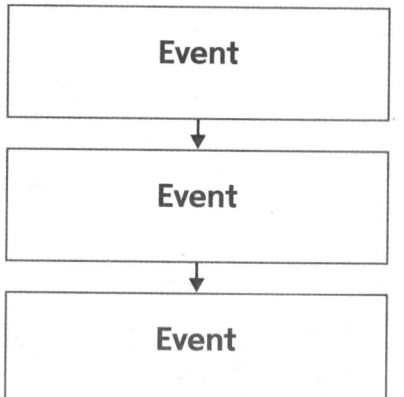

Event

↓

Event

↓

Event

CHECK IN 1 2 3 4

Draft

Descriptive Details Authors use rich details to describe the people, setting, and events of their narratives. Appropriate descriptions are those that help readers imagine how things look, sound, smell, and feel. Read the first paragraph on page 21 of *Gary the Dreamer* in the **Literature Anthology**. Use text evidence to answer the questions below.

How does Gary Soto describe the sound of the water?

_____

_____

What does he think the bubbles looked like?

_____

_____

Think about putting bubbles on your face to make a beard. Write two words that describe how the bubbles might feel.

_____

_____

Write a Draft Use your Sequence of Events chart to write a draft of your narrative in your writer's notebook. Add descriptive details to tell about the people, setting, and events. Use transitional words and phrases to show the sequence of events.

CHECK IN 1 › 2 › 3 › 4 ›

Revise

Sentence Fluency Authors use a variety of sentence types and lengths to make their writing more interesting to read. They also include dialogue to show what people say to one another.

Reread the last two paragraphs on page 15 of *Gary the Dreamer* in the **Literature Anthology**. Talk with a partner about the variety of sentence types and dialogue. Write about it here.

_____

_____

_____

Revise It's time to revise your writing. Read your draft and look for places where you might

- use a variety of sentence types and lengths

- include dialogue

Circle two sentences from your draft that you can change. Revise and write them here.

1 _____

2 _____

CHECK IN   1   2   3   4

Peer Conferences

Review a Draft Listen carefully as a partner reads his or her draft aloud. Tell what you like about the draft. Use these sentence starters to help you discuss your partner's draft.

I like this part because it made me feel . . .

Can this sentence be . . .

Add another detail to describe . . .

Partner Feedback After you take turns giving each other feedback, write one of the suggestions from your partner that you will use in your revision.

_____

_____

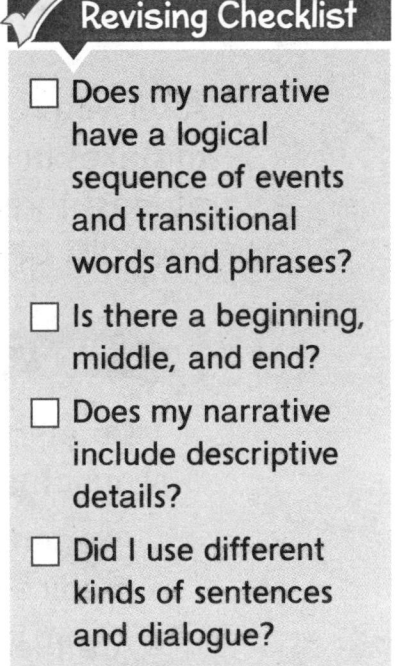

Revising Checklist

- ☐ Does my narrative have a logical sequence of events and transitional words and phrases?
- ☐ Is there a beginning, middle, and end?
- ☐ Does my narrative include descriptive details?
- ☐ Did I use different kinds of sentences and dialogue?

Revision After you finish your peer conference, use the Revising Checklist to help you make your narrative better. Remember to use the rubric on page 97 to help you with your revision.

Digital Tools

For more information about how to have peer conferences, watch "Peer Conferencing." Go to **my.mheducation.com**.

Edit and Proofread

After you revise your personal narrative, proofread it to find any mistakes in grammar, spelling, and punctuation. Read your draft at least three times. This will help you catch any mistakes. Use the checklist below to edit your sentences.

Tech Tip

If you wrote your draft on a computer, print it out. It's easier to check for mistakes on paper than on a screen.

Editing Checklist

- ☐ Do all sentences begin with a capital letter and end with a punctuation mark?
- ☐ Are sentences complete sentences with a subject and predicate?
- ☐ Are there any sentence fragments?
- ☐ Are all words spelled correctly?

Grammar Connections

When you proofread your draft for punctuation mistakes, remember that you should always capitalize the pronoun *I*, as in, "At lunch, I ate pizza and carrot sticks."

List two mistakes that you found as you proofread your narrative.

1 _____

_____

_____

2 _____

_____

_____

Publish, Present, and Evaluate

Publishing When you publish your writing, you create a neat final copy that is free of mistakes. If you are not using a computer, write legibly in print or cursive.

Presentation When you are ready to present, practice your presentation. Use the Presenting Checklist.

Evaluate After you publish, use the rubric to evaluate your writing.

What did you do successfully? _____

_____

What needs more work? _____

_____

✓ **Presenting Checklist**

☐ Look at the audience.

☐ Speak slowly and clearly.

☐ Speak loudly enough so everyone can hear you.

☐ Answer questions thoughtfully.

Turn to page 89. Fill in the bars to show what you learned.

4	3	2	1
• tells about a personal experience and includes thoughts and feelings • presents events in the correct order • uses a variety of sentences	• tells about a personal experience and includes some feelings • presents events in the correct order • varies sentences	• tells about a personal experience • includes events that are told out of order • uses only simple sentences	• does not tell about a personal experience • tells events out of order and is confusing • sentences are choppy

My Goal I can write an opinion essay.

Expert Model

Features of an Opinion Essay

An opinion essay is a kind of argumentative text. An opinion essay

- clearly tells the writer's opinion in the opening and conclusion
- includes reasons for the opinion, such as facts and examples, that are supported by details from research
- tries to convince readers to agree with the writer's opinion

Literature Anthology: pages 50–53

Analyze an Expert Model Reread page 51 of "Protecting Our Parks" in the **Literature Anthology**. Use text evidence to answer these questions.

How do you know the author thinks it is important to protect

national parks? _____

_____

_____

How does the author try to convince readers that national parks

need more protection? _____

_____

_____

Word Wise

"Protecting Our Parks" gives points for and counterpoints against the argument that national parks should be open to all visitors. An opinion essay usually picks one claim and gives facts and opinions to support the argument.

Plan: Choose Your Topic

Brainstorm With a partner, think of some national parks or landmarks. How might visiting these places help you learn about our country? Use these sentence starters to talk about your ideas.

A national park or landmark I know is . . .

One reason to visit this place is . . .

Writing Prompt Choose one of the parks or landmarks you discussed as your topic for an opinion essay. You will need to convince your readers that this is an important place to visit to learn about the United States.

I will write about _____

Purpose and Audience An author's purpose is the main reason for writing. Your audience is who will be reading what you write.

The reason I am writing about this topic is _____

_____

_____

_____

Plan Think about what you want your readers to learn about the place you are writing about. Why should they visit? Ask yourself questions and answer them in your writer's notebook.

CHECK IN 1 > 2 > 3 > 4

Plan: Research

Identify Relevant Information You will need to research your topic before you write. Use encyclopedias, websites, and books to gather information about your national park or landmark. Ask an adult to help you plan your research and choose your sources. Remember that it is important that the facts and examples in your sources are relevant, or related, to your topic.

Work with an adult to write three steps in your research plan.

1. _____

2. _____

3. _____

List the titles of two sources you will use here.

_____

_____

 **Chart** In your writer's notebook, make a Central Idea and Relevant Details chart. Take notes and fill in your chart with your opinion and three relevant details that support it.

Quick Tip

Remember that your purpose for writing is to convince your readers that your national park is an important place to learn about the United States. The information you find in your sources should support the reasons you include in your essay.

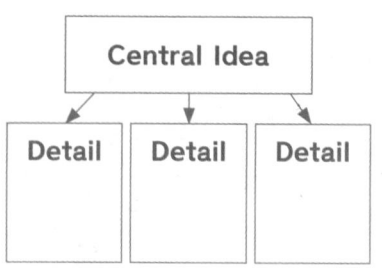

CHECK IN 1 2 3 4

Draft

Fact and Opinion Writers use facts to support their opinions. Facts are true and can be proved. Opinions are beliefs that might or might not be true. In the example below from "Protecting Our Parks," the author uses facts to support an opinion.

> The National Park Service thinks that people should be able to visit America's parks and landmarks. Their mission is to protect land so that it can be enjoyed by everyone. They want families to hike the trails, observe the animals, and learn about our country's history. But visitors need bathrooms, parking lots, and places to eat.

Now use the above paragraph as a model to write about the park or landmark you chose for your topic. Remember to use facts.

_____

_____

_____

_____

_____

 **Write a Draft** Look over your Central Idea and Relevant Details chart. Use it to write a draft in your writer's notebook. Make sure you clearly state your opinion and support it with facts. Remember to include a conclusion at the end of your essay.

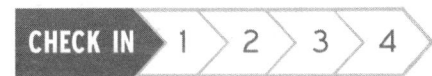
CHECK IN 1 2 3 4

Revise

Strong Opening Opinion essays that have a strong opening begin by clearly stating the writer's opinion. They also grab the reader's attention so that the reader will want to keep reading.

Reread the first two paragraphs of "Protecting Our Parks" on page 51 of the **Literature Anthology**. Talk with a partner about how the author grabs your attention. Write about it here.

_____

_____

_____

Revise It's time to revise your writing. Read your draft and think about ways you might

- state your opinion more clearly

- include facts that grab the reader's attention

Circle two sentences in your draft that you can change. Revise and write them here.

1 _____

_____

2 _____

_____

Peer Conferences

Review a Draft Listen carefully as a partner reads his or her draft aloud. Tell what you like about the draft. Use these sentence starters to help you discuss your partner's draft.

I like the way you started your essay because . . .

Add another fact here to . . .

You did/did not convince me because . . .

I have a question about . . .

Partner Feedback After you take turns giving each other feedback, write one of your partner's suggestions that you will use in your revision.

_____

_____

_____

_____

Revision After you finish your peer conference, use the Revising Checklist to figure out what you can change to make your opinion essay better. Remember to use the rubric on page 105 to help with your revision.

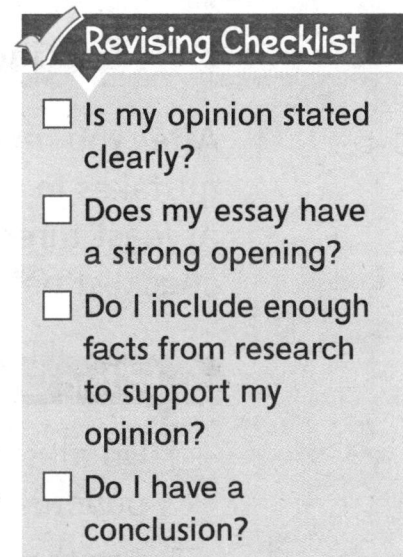

✔ Revising Checklist

☐ Is my opinion stated clearly?

☐ Does my essay have a strong opening?

☐ Do I include enough facts from research to support my opinion?

☐ Do I have a conclusion?

💻 Tech Tip

The program you use to write your draft on a computer should include a thesaurus. The thesaurus will help you find synonyms for words you might want to replace. Using new words instead of repeating old ones can make your essay more interesting to read.

Edit and Proofread

After you revise your opinion essay, proofread it to find any mistakes in grammar, spelling, and punctuation. Read your draft at least three times. This will help you catch any mistakes. Use the checklist below to edit your sentences.

✓ Editing Checklist

- ☐ Do all sentences start with a capital letter and end with a punctuation mark?
- ☐ Are the names of specific parks or landmarks capitalized?
- ☐ Are both simple and compound sentences used?
- ☐ Are all words spelled correctly?

List two mistakes that you found as you proofread your opinion essay.

1 _____

_____

_____

2 _____

_____

_____

Grammar Connections

When you proofread your draft for mistakes, remember that using a combination of both simple and compound sentences will make your essay more interesting. A simple sentence is a complete sentence made of a subject and a verb. A compound sentence is made of two simple sentences joined by words such as *and*, *but*, *or*, and *so*.

Publish, Present, and Evaluate

Publishing When you publish your writing, you create a neat final copy that is free of mistakes. If you are not using a computer, use your best handwriting. Write legibly in print or cursive.

Presentation When you are ready to present, practice your presentation. Use the Presenting Checklist.

Evaluate After you publish, use the rubric to evaluate your writing.

✓ Presenting Checklist

- ☐ Look at the audience.
- ☐ Speak slowly and clearly.
- ☐ Present your opinion and supporting facts with confidence.
- ☐ Answer questions thoughtfully.

What did you do well? _____

_____

What could use some improvement? _____

_____

Turn to page 89. Fill in the bars to show what you learned.

4	3	2	1
• claim is clearly stated in a strong opening • includes several supporting facts • very few spelling, grammar, or punctuation errors	• claim is clearly stated • includes supporting facts • some spelling, grammar, or punctuation errors	• claim is somewhat unclear • includes few supporting facts • several spelling, grammar, and punctuation errors	• claim is not stated • includes only one supporting fact • many spelling, grammar, and punctuation errors

My Goal

I can read and understand social studies texts.

TAKE NOTES

Take notes and annotate as you read the passages "Steel Drums of the Caribbean" and "Career Day."

Look for the answer to the question. *What is one way people of the Caribbean share their culture?*

_____

_____

_____

_____

_____

_____

PASSAGE 1

EXPOSITORY TEXT

STEEL DRUMS OF THE CARIBBEAN

Amazing sounds can come from surprising places, such as a hammered steel drum.

In the Caribbean Sea, seven miles from Venezuela, lies an island called Trinidad. It is the birthplace of the steel drum. Also known as a steel pan, this musical instrument is very popular in the Caribbean.

Traditionally, steel drums are made from old oil barrels. The oil barrels are cut and hammered to create notes. The drums are played with two rubber-tipped sticks. There are many different types of steel drums. They each make different sounds, like different musical instruments. The notes of a particular "instrument" are sometimes spread across two or more drums.

It is exciting to watch steel pan musicians in action. One player may play two to nine drums at once. The player dances the whole time without missing a beat.

There are hundreds of steel bands in the Caribbean. Big bands can have up to 100 players and 150 steel drums. The bands usually play calypso or soca music. These popular music styles were created in the Caribbean.

No one knows exactly how the steel drum was invented. Winston "Spree" Simon was the first steel drum celebrity. In 1950, he gave the first pan recital in Trinidad. He played sambas, calypsos, and classical European music. The audience loved it. One year later, he performed in London. He was a surprise hit!

Today, steel bands perform around the world. Watch for the next time a steel band comes to your town.

 **PASSAGE 2** REALISTIC FICTION

Career Day

Mia and her dad were in front of Mia's school. "You're quiet. Aren't you excited about Career Day?" asked Dad.

Mia looked down at her sneakers. "I guess so," she sighed. Students streamed through the big glass doors, chattering excitedly. Dad unloaded a large container from their car.

"Yesterday I told my new friend, Sofia, that you were going to talk about steel pan music. She gave me a funny look and left the room," Mia said. "I don't think she likes music."

Dad laughed. "Sofia doesn't know that a steel pan is a drum. Don't worry, it will be a nice surprise."

Mia's teacher, Ms. Pickles, greeted them enthusiastically. "Mr. Ray teaches music history," Ms. Pickles told the class. "Today he will talk to us about music from the Caribbean."

TAKE NOTES

TAKE NOTES

_____

_____

_____

_____

_____

_____

_____

_____

_____

_____

_____

_____

_____

_____

_____

_____

Mia's classmates were quiet as mice while Mia's dad spoke. He explained that music is very important in Caribbean culture. He described festivals around the Caribbean. He spoke about reggae from Jamaica, compas from Haiti, and salsa from Cuba.

"I could talk all day, but let's have a demonstration. Steel drums come from Trinidad, where I'm from. A steel band might have a hundred steel pans, as we call them. We have just one steel pan here today, but a very special player. Are you ready, Mia?"

Mia came to the front of the class with two rubber-tipped sticks. She rolled out calypso melodies that had the class swaying in their seats. They cheered when she finished.

"Play another!" Sofia called out from the front row. She clapped louder than anyone.

COMPARE THE PASSAGES

Review your notes from the two passages. Then create a Venn diagram like the one below. Use your notes and the diagram to show how what you learned in the passages is alike and different.

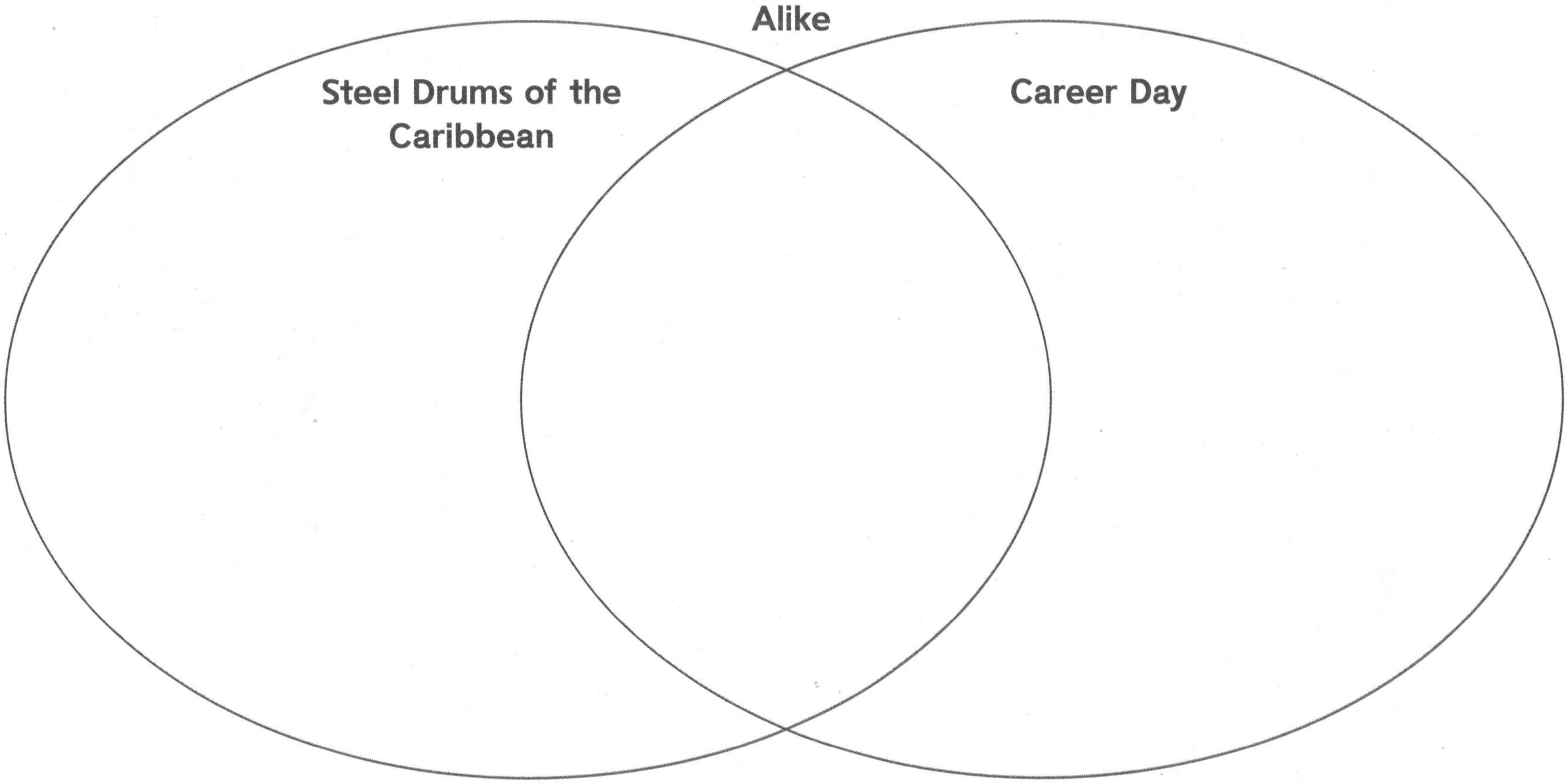

Alike

Steel Drums of the Caribbean

Career Day

Synthesize Information

Think about what you learned from both texts. How can music help you learn more about Caribbean culture? What are some other ways you can learn about another culture?

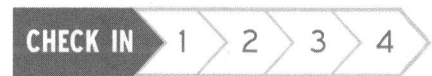

LABEL A MAP

Maps can help us understand where the places we read about are located. This map can help you understand more about the places mentioned in "Steel Drums of the Caribbean." Use the word bank of place names to label each country and U.S. territory in the map below. Use an atlas or a globe for help.

Word Bank
The Bahamas
Cuba
Dominican Republic
Haiti
Jamaica
Puerto Rico
Trinidad and Tobago

THE CARIBBEAN

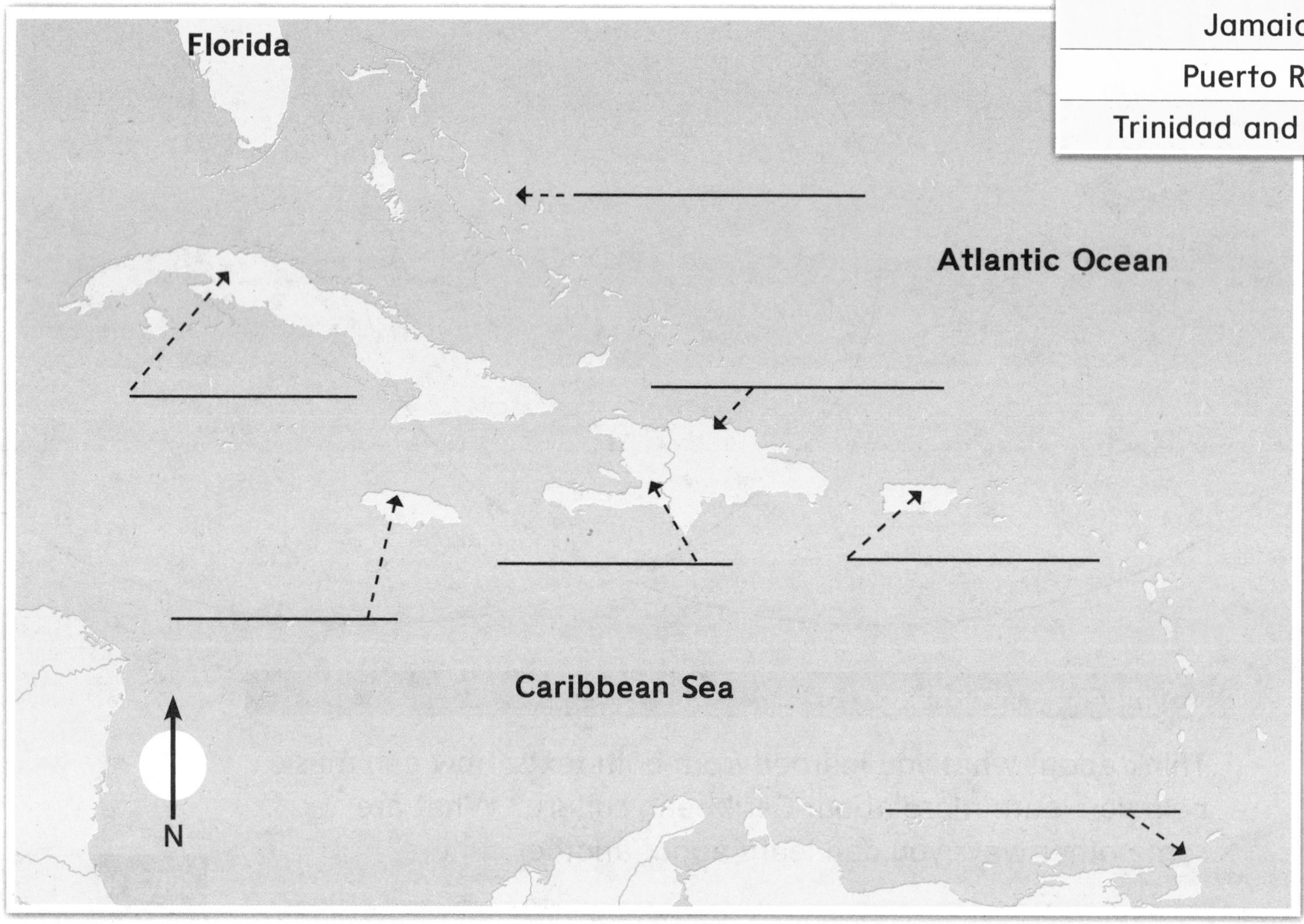
Florida
Atlantic Ocean
Caribbean Sea
N

dikobraziy/Shutterstock

CREATE A CARIBBEAN FACT SHEET

Look at the Caribbean map you just completed. Pick three Caribbean places you labeled to research. Use the chart below to record facts about each country or territory you chose. A sample for one country is shown.

COUNTRY/ TERRITORY	CAPITAL CITY	TYPE OF MUSIC	FAMOUS MUSICIANS	FESTIVALS
Haiti	Port-au-Prince	compas	Nemours Jean-Baptiste, Tabou Combo	Carnival, New Year's Day/ Independence Day

After you finish your fact sheet, discuss with your partner some questions you have about the Caribbean region. Make a plan to explore the questions that interest you most.

My Goal I can read and understand science texts.

TAKE NOTES

Take notes and annotate as you read the passages "Saving Desert Treasures" and "Protecting the Pronghorn."

Look for an answer to the question. *How do people help protect the environment?*

_____

_____

_____

_____

_____

_____

_____

PASSAGE 1 · EXPOSITORY TEXT

Saving DESERT TREASURES

For thousands of years, Bighorn sheep lived in the Sonoran Desert. However, more people moved to this part of Arizona in the early 1900s and built gold mines. The sheep began to disappear. A man named Major Frederick R. Burnham, who loved the desert and its animals, noticed what was happening. What could be done?

Major Burnham asked the Boy Scouts for help, as they often worked to protect the environment. Other groups joined in the cause. In 1936, they started holding meetings and radio talks. They even held a poster contest to "save the Bighorns." Their campaign worked! On April 2, 1939, a large area became a refuge.

Today that area is called the Kofa National Wildlife Refuge. It is 665,400 acres. That is almost twice as big as the city of Houston, Texas! Besides Bighorn, the refuge is home to many other special plants and animals.

The saguaro cactus is one such plant. These cacti only grow in the Sonoran Desert. They like the desert's heat, but they also need some rain to grow. The Sonoran Desert's summer rainy season is just right for the saguaro.

The saguaro grows very slowly. It can take ten years to grow one inch! As it grows, it becomes a column. It does not start growing arms until it is 100 years old.

This cactus is good at surviving dry times. Its long taproot draws up deep water. Surface rainwater goes into its many shallow roots. A saguaro can store water for a long time. Its body has ribs that swell to make room for stored water. Its waxy skin keeps water inside. Its sharp spines scare off water-seeking animals.

Once people went to the Kofa National Wildlife Refuge to find gold. Now they come to enjoy the Bighorn sheep and Saguaro cacti. The Refuge is still full of treasures.

Saguaro cacti in the Sonoran Desert.

Pete Ryan/National Geographic/Getty Images

TAKE NOTES

_____

_____

_____

_____

_____

_____

_____

_____

_____

_____

_____

_____

PASSAGE 2

EXPOSITORY TEXT

PROTECTING THE PRONGHORN

One of the most endangered mammals lives in Arizona's Sonoran Desert. The Sonoran pronghorn have lived here for thousands of years. Now fewer than 200 still roam free.

Tony Attanasio/iStock/Getty Images

Sonoran pronghorn live in Arizona and Mexico. They can be spotted in the Kofa National Wildlife Refuge, but not easily. They are called the "desert ghost" because they are so shy. When spooked, they can run 60 miles per hour.

The Sonoran pronghorn is about three feet high at its shoulder. Males can weigh 130 pounds, while females weigh about 110 pounds. All pronghorn have horns, but the males' horns are much longer. They mostly eat desert plants and fruits. Fruit gives them water during dry times.

Many groups are working to protect the pronghorn. The U.S. Fish and Wildlife Service is one of them. They work to increase the pronghorn's numbers. They are partnering with Mexican conservationists. They hope that someday the Sonoran pronghorn will no longer be endangered.

COMPARE THE PASSAGES

Review your notes from the two passages. Then create a Venn diagram like the one below. Use your notes and the diagram to write how information in the two passages is alike and different.

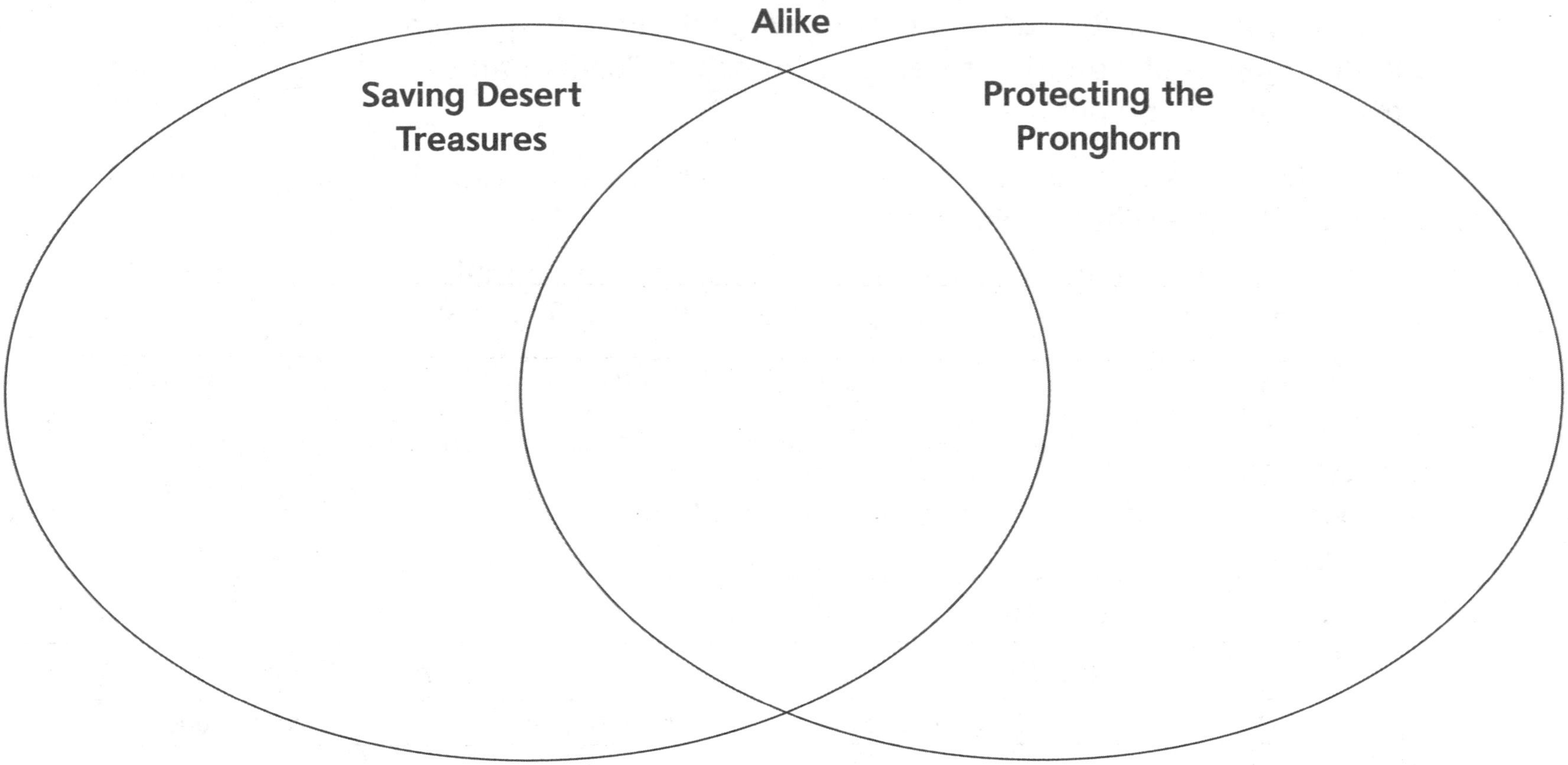

Alike

Saving Desert Treasures

Protecting the Pronghorn

Synthesize Information

Think about what you learned from both texts. How has the Kofa National Wildlife Preserve helped the environment? What might have happened if the preserve was never created?

CHECK IN 1 2 3 4

HOW DOES A CACTUS STORE WATER?

Plants need water and soil to live. Roots hold up the plant and keep it in place. The roots also draw water from the soil that the plant needs to live. Plants use energy from the Sun, air, and water to make their own food.

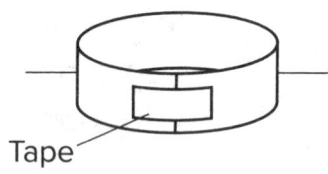

Tape

You've read about the Saguaro cactus. When it rains, It can store large amounts of water in its stem and branches. Conduct an experiment to find out how.

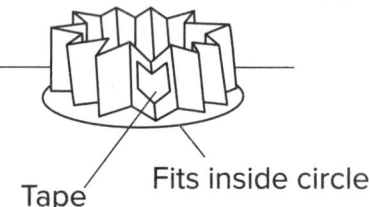

Tape   Fits inside circle

- Gather the materials: two paper strips, one 5- by 1-inches and one 10- by 1-inches; tape; dried beans

- Make a round stem: Tape the ends of the short strip to make a round "stem" as shown. Make sure it fits on the circle, at right.

Fit round stem and cactus stem here.

- Make a cactus stem: Fold the long strip like a fan and tape closed. Make sure it fits on the circle.

- Estimate: How many beans can the round stem hold? The cactus stem? Test each stem, one at a time.

- Test each stem, one at a time. Record your estimates and observations on the chart.

Round Stem		Cactus Stem	
My Estimate	Observations	My Estimate	Observations

COLLABORATE

Discuss your results with a partner. Let's say the beans are water. Which stem can store more? What helps a Saguaro cactus stem store water?

Reflect on Your Learning

 **Talk About It** Reflect on what you learned in this unit. Then talk with a partner about how you did.

I am really proud of how I can _____

_____

_____

_____

Something I need to work more on is _____

_____

_____

_____

Share a goal you have with a partner.

 **My Goal** Set a goal for Unit 2. In your reader's notebook, write about what you can do to get there.

Build Knowledge

BALLOT BOX

Build Vocabulary

Write new words you learned about government. Draw lines and circles for the words you write.

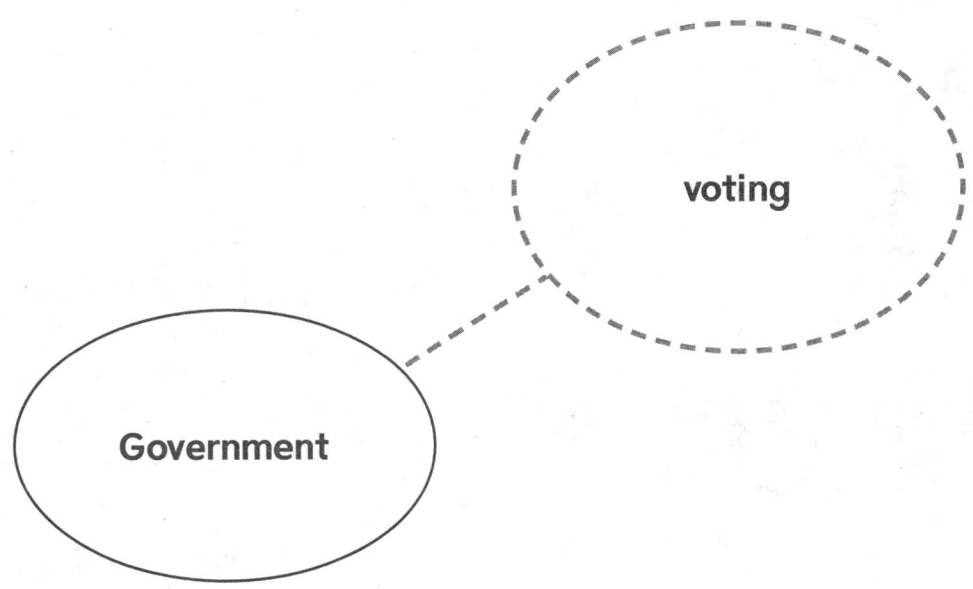

voting

Government

Go online to **my.mheducation.com** and read the "Let's Vote On It" Blast. Think about why learning about government and voting is important. Then blast back your response.

Richard Hutchings/Corbis Documentary/Getty Images

Think about what you already know. Wherever you are is okay. Fill in the bars.

What I Know Now

Key

1 =	I do not understand.
2 =	I understand but need more practice.
3 =	I understand.
4 =	I understand and can teach someone.

I can read and understand expository text.

1 > 2 > 3 > 4

I can use text evidence to respond to expository text.

1 > 2 > 3 > 4

I know how people make government work.

1 > 2 > 3 > 4

 **STOP** You will come back to the next page later.

Think about what you learned. Fill in the bars. Keep doing your best!

What I Learned

I can read and understand expository text.

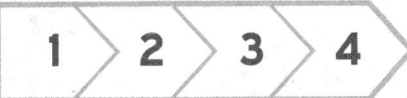

1 > 2 > 3 > 4

I can use text evidence to respond to expository text.

1 > 2 > 3 > 4

I know how people make government work.

1 > 2 > 3 > 4

SHARED READ

My Goal I can read and understand expository text.

TAKE NOTES

As you read, make note of interesting words and important information.

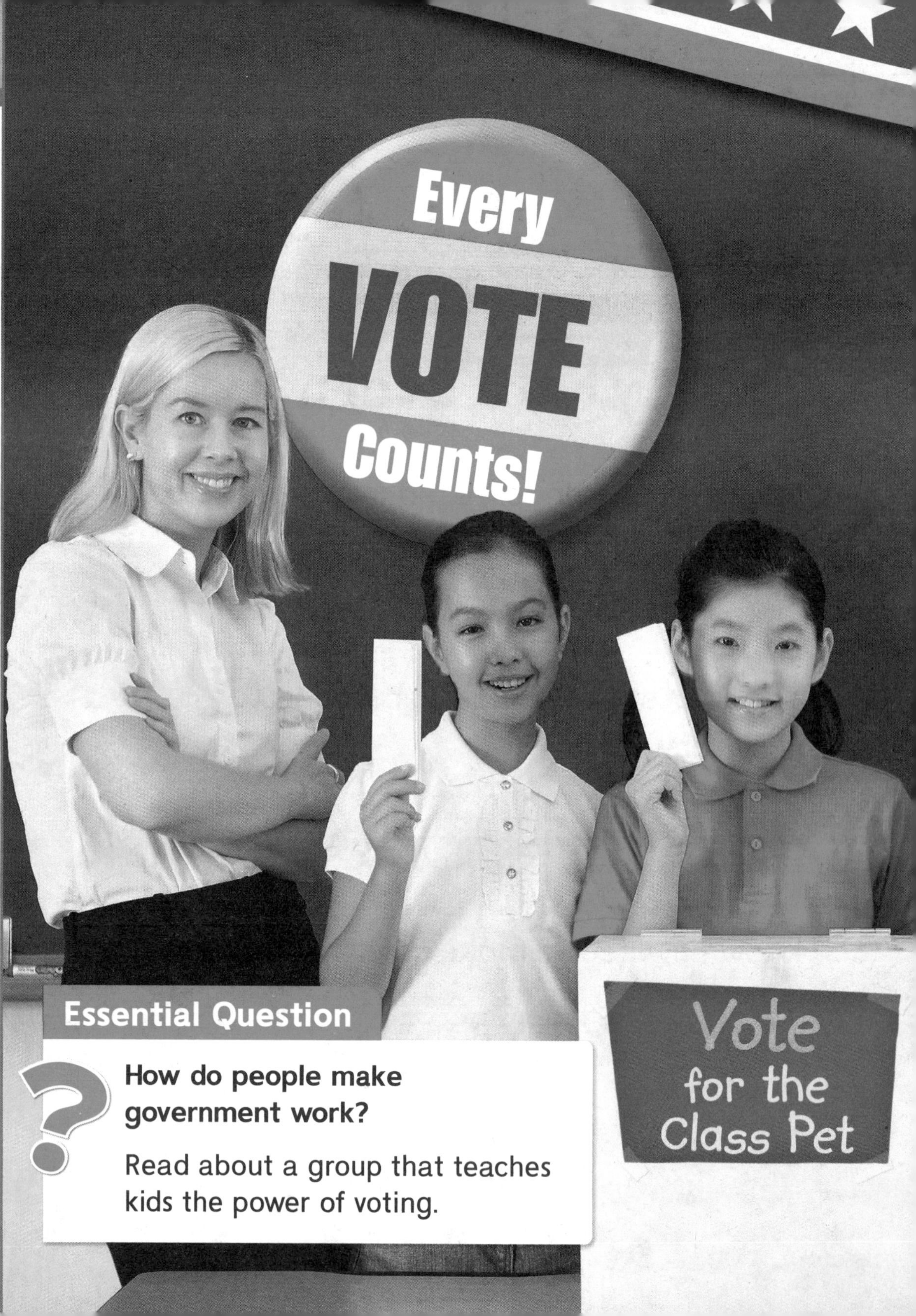
Every
VOTE
Counts!
Vote
for the
Class Pet

Essential Question

How do people make government work?

Read about a group that teaches kids the power of voting.

Have you ever voted? Maybe you voted to choose a class pet. Maybe your family voted on which movie to see. If you have ever voted, then you know how good it feels. Voting is important. It tells people what you think.

Many years ago, the leaders of our country wanted to know what people thought, too. They wrote a plan for our **government**. It is called the Constitution. It gives men and women in the United States the right to vote.

Each year, people who are eighteen years and older pick new leaders. They also vote on new laws. Voting gives Americans the power to choose.

FIND TEXT EVIDENCE

Read

Paragraph 1

Author's Claim

What does the author think is important about voting? **Draw a box around** text evidence.

Paragraphs 2–3

Reread

What is the Constitution? **Circle** text evidence that tells what it is. **Underline** text that tells what it does. Write what it does here.

_____

_____

_____

_____

_____

Reread

Author's Craft

How does the author help you understand the role voting plays in our country?

Read

Paragraph 1

Author's Claim

How does the author feel about people not voting?

_____

_____

_____

_____

Draw a box around text evidence.

Paragraph 2

Headings

What is the heading of this section? Write it here.

_____

_____

Underline text evidence that tells what Kids Voting USA does to teach kids to vote.

Teaching Kids to Vote

Did you know that only about six out of every ten Americans vote? That's sad. Some people think that voting is too hard. They are unsure where to go to vote. They think it takes too much time. Now, a group called Kids Voting USA is trying to **convince** everyone to vote.

Kids Voting USA teaches kids that voting is important. The group gives teachers lessons to use in their classrooms. First, kids read stories and do fun activities about government. They also learn how to choose and **elect** a good leader.

Election Day is here!

First we sign in.

Next, kids talk with their families. They reread stories about **candidates**. These are the people who want to be chosen as leaders. Families discuss their ideas and make **decisions**. That way, when it's time to vote, kids know whom they want to vote for.

On Election Day, kids get to vote just like adults. They use ballots like the ones in real elections. A ballot is a special form with the names of candidates on it. Kids mark their choices on the ballot. Then they put the ballot into a special box. Finally, all the votes are counted and recounted. The winners are **announced**, and everyone knows who won.

Then we mark a ballot.

Finally we vote!

Richard Hutchings/Corbis Documentary/Getty Images

FIND TEXT EVIDENCE

> Read

Paragraph 1
Reread
Underline two things that help kids make decisions about whom to vote for.

Paragraph 2
Prefixes
Draw a box around *recounted*. Write the prefix here.

_____

What does *recounted* mean?

_____

_____

_____

_____

> Reread

Author's Craft

How does the author help you understand what a ballot is?

FIND TEXT EVIDENCE

Read

Paragraph 1

Reread

Underline how voting helps kids. Why does Kids Voting USA want kids to vote now?

_____

_____

Paragraph 2

Author's Claim

What does the author think about voting?

_____

_____

Circle text evidence to support your answer.

Reread

Author's Craft

How does the author use the caption to help you understand how kids are learning to vote?

Vote Now

Voting helps kids learn how to be **independent** and think for themselves. It also gives them the power to share how they feel. Kids Voting USA wants kids to vote now. There's a good reason. They **estimate** that when these kids grow up, more of them will vote.

In about ten years, kids your age will be old enough to vote. You will have the power to help elect great leaders and make new laws. Isn't that exciting?

Elections are held in many schools to teach kids how to vote.

This bar graph shows the results of a class election. Which pet was the favorite?

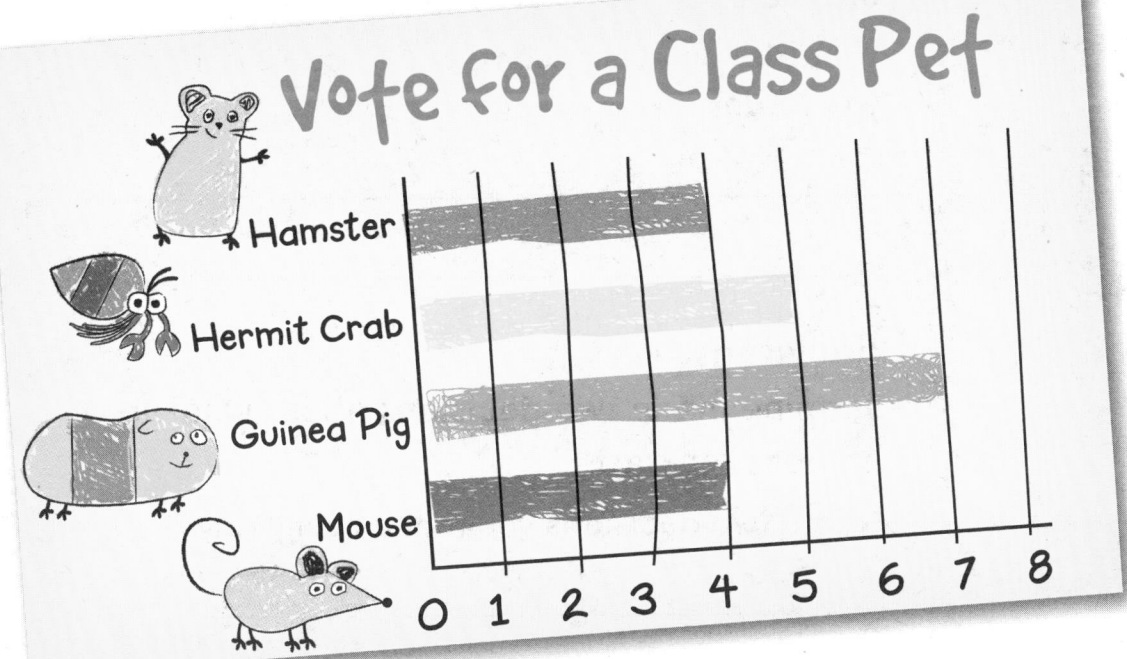

Vote for a Class Pet

Hamster
Hermit Crab
Guinea Pig
Mouse
0 1 2 3 4 5 6 7 8

FIND TEXT EVIDENCE

Read
Paragraph 1
Reread
What does the bar graph show?

_____

_____

_____

Underline text evidence.

Bar Graphs

Look at the bar graph. **Circle** the pets in the class election. Which pet got the most votes?

_____

How many votes did it get?

_____

Reread
Author's Craft

How does the bar graph help you understand more about voting?

Summarize

Use your notes and think about why voting is important. Summarize the text using the central idea and relevant details.

Vocabulary

Use the sentences to talk with a partner about each word. Then answer the questions.

announced

The teacher **announced** the winner of the election.

What is something that your teacher has announced?

_____

_____

candidates

Andrew was happy to be one of the **candidates** for class president.

What are some things candidates do before an election?

_____

_____

convince

Amir tried to **convince** his friend to play baseball.

What is something someone tried to convince you to do?

_____

_____

decisions

Jasmine made two **decisions** about what to eat for breakfast.

Name two decisions you make every day.

_____

_____

elect

The players voted to **elect** a team captain.

What is another word for *elect*?

_____

_____

Build Your Word List Reread the second paragraph on page 123. Draw a box around the word *right*. Look up the definitions of the word *right* using a dictionary. Use context clues to figure out the meaning. Write a sentence using *right* in your reader's notebook.

estimate

Shauna tried to **estimate**, or guess, the weight of her cat.

What does it mean to estimate something?

_____

_____

government

Miguel went to city hall to learn about his local **government**.

Write down one thing that your local government does.

_____

_____

independent

It's good to be **independent** and do things on your own.

How can you be more independent at home?

_____

Prefixes

A prefix is a word part added to the beginning of a word. It changes the meaning of the word. The prefix *un-* means "not." The prefix *re-* means "again."

🔍 FIND TEXT EVIDENCE

In the first paragraph on page 125, I see the sentence "They reread stories about candidates." *The word* reread *has the prefix* re-. *I know the prefix* re- *means "again." The word* reread *must mean "read again."*

They reread stories about candidates.

Your Turn Find the word *unsure* on page 124. Use the prefix to figure out the meaning of the word. Write it here.

unsure _____

CHECK IN ▷ 1 ⟩ 2 ⟩ 3 ⟩ 4 ⟩

Reread

Stop and think about the text as you read. Do you understand what you are reading? Does it make sense? Reread to make sure you understand.

🔍 FIND TEXT EVIDENCE

Do you understand why the author thinks voting is important? Reread the first part of page 123.

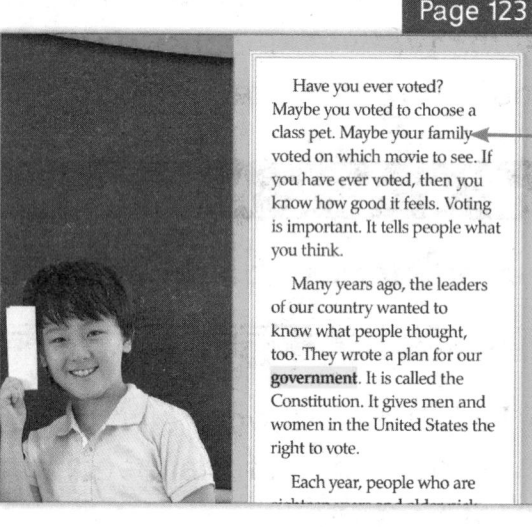

Page 123

Have you ever voted? Maybe you voted to choose a class pet. Maybe your family voted on which movie to see. If you have ever voted, then you know how good it feels. Voting is important. It tells people what you think.

Many years ago, the leaders of our country wanted to know what people thought, too. They wrote a plan for our **government**. It is called the Constitution. It gives men and women in the United States the right to vote.

Each year, people who are

I read that voting is a way to tell people what you think. It is a way for people to choose new laws and leaders. Now I understand why the author thinks voting is important.

Your Turn How does Kids Voting USA teach kids to vote? Reread pages 124 and 125. Then write the answer here.

_____

_____

_____

CHECK IN 1 2 3 4

Headings and Bar Graphs

"Every Vote Counts!" is an **expository text**. An expository text

- gives facts and information about a topic
- has headings that tell what a section is about
- includes text features, such as headings and bar graphs

FIND TEXT EVIDENCE

I can tell "Every Vote Counts!" is an expository text. It gives facts about voting. It also has headings and a bar graph.

Page 127

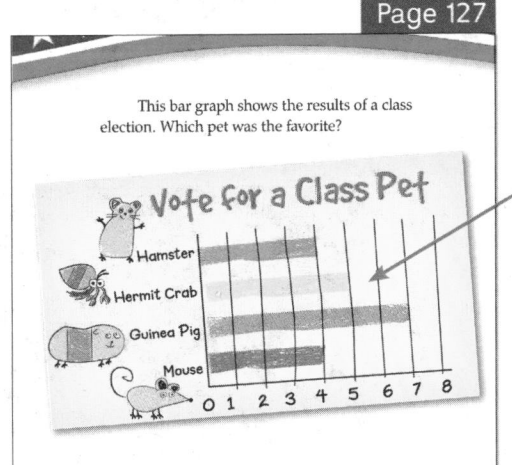

This bar graph shows the results of a class election. Which pet was the favorite?

Headings

A heading tells what a section of text is mostly about.

Bar Graphs

A bar graph is a special kind of text feature. It helps you understand and compare numbers and information in a quick and easy way.

Your Turn Look at the bar graph on page 127. Talk with a partner about something you learned. Write it here.

_____

_____

_____

CHECK IN 1 ⟩ 2 ⟩ 3 ⟩ 4

Author's Claim

A claim is something an author believes to be true. Authors support their claims with reasons and evidence. To identify an author's claim, look for details that tell what the author thinks and feels. Then look for what the details have in common.

 FIND TEXT EVIDENCE

What does the author think about voting? I can reread and look for details that tell me what the author thinks.

Details
The title of the text is "Every Vote Counts!"
The author thinks it's sad that only six out of every ten Americans vote.
Voting gives Americans the right to choose.

Details help you figure out the author's claim.

Author's Claim
Voting is important. Everyone should vote.

 **Your Turn** Reread "Every Vote Counts!" Find details that show how the author feels about Kids Voting USA. Add details in the graphic organizer. What is the author's claim? Do you agree with it?

CHECK IN 1 2 3 4

Details

↓

Author's Claim

Respond to Reading

COLLABORATE Talk about the prompt below. Use your notes and evidence from the text to support your answer.

Why should everyone exercise their right to vote?

_____

_____

_____

_____

_____

_____

_____

_____

_____

_____

_____

Quick Tip

Use these sentence starters to talk about the prompt.

Everyone should vote because . . .

One reason voting is important is . . .

Grammar Connections

Remember to use complete sentences. A complete sentence says who or what is doing something and what they are doing.

A statement tells something and ends with a period. A question asks something. It ends with a question mark.

CHECK IN 1 ⟩ 2 ⟩ 3 ⟩ 4

Workers in Your Community

COLLABORATE

A thank-you note is a way to let people know you're thankful for something they did. Follow the research process to learn about a group or individual who works in your community's local government. Then write a thank-you letter. Work with a partner.

Step 1 Set a Goal Brainstorm a list of groups and individuals who work in your local government. Choose one you would like to learn more about.

Step 2 Identify Sources Use books and reliable websites to learn more about your group or individual.

Step 3 Find and Record Information Use your sources to take notes on information about what your group or individual does to help your community. Remember to cite your sources.

Step 4 Organize and Combine Information Plan your thank-you note. Think of the reasons why you are thankful for the job your group or individual does for your community.

Step 5 Create and Present Use your notes to write your thank-you note. Include a greeting at the beginning of your note and a closing at the end. Use a friendly, informal tone.

Quick Tip

The appropriate tone, or attitude, of a thank-you note is friendly and informal. This means using words and phrases that you use in everyday conversation.

Dear Ms. James,

Thank you for taking such good care of the new baseball field at Turner Park. My friends and I like playing ball there.

Sincerely,
Akilah

CHECK IN 1 2 3 4

Vote!

? **How does the author help you understand that voting is important?**

Literature Anthology: pages 100–119

Talk About It Reread **Literature Anthology** page 104 and look at the illustrations. Talk with a partner about how important each person's vote is.

Cite Text Evidence What clues in the text and illustrations help you see that every vote counts? Write them in the chart.

Evaluate Information

As you read, evaluate details to identify key ideas. Ask: *What details does the author use to help me understand how she feels about voting?* Focus on clues that help you see why voting is important.

Text Evidence	Illustration Clues	How It Helps

Write The author helps me understand how voting is important by

_____

_____

_____

CHECK IN 1 2 3 4

How does the author use illustrations and speech bubbles to help you understand how people vote?

Talk About It Analyze the illustrations and speech bubbles on **Literature Anthology** pages 112 and 113. Talk with a partner about what it is like to vote.

Cite Text Evidence How do the pictures and words help you understand the voting process? Write evidence in the chart.

Illustrations Show	Speech Bubbles Explain

Write Illustrations and speech bubbles help me understand _____

_____

_____

_____

Quick Tip

Use these sentence starters to talk about how to vote.

The illustrations show . . .

The speech bubbles help me understand . . .

Make Inferences

The illustrations show curtains surrounding each voting booth. Use text evidence and make an inference, or conclusion, to figure out why the voting booths have curtains.

CHECK IN 1 2 3 4

How does the author help you understand what happens at a swearing-in ceremony?

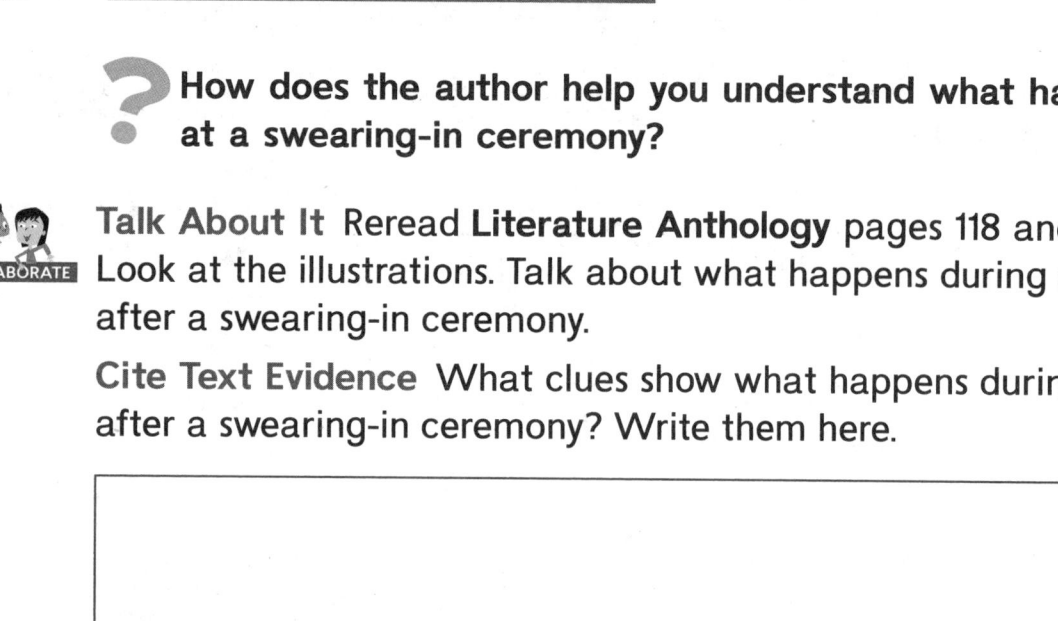

Talk About It Reread **Literature Anthology** pages 118 and 119. Look at the illustrations. Talk about what happens during and after a swearing-in ceremony.

Cite Text Evidence What clues show what happens during and after a swearing-in ceremony? Write them here.

Quick Tip

When I reread, I can look for text evidence to answer questions.

Make Inferences

An inference is a conclusion based on facts. The author says that the new mayor won't please all the people all the time. Make an inference about which group of voters is more likely to be happy with her and which is more likely to be unhappy.

Write The author helps me understand what happens by

CHECK IN 1 2 3 4

Respond to Reading

COLLABORATE Talk about the prompt below. Use your notes and evidence from the text to support your answer.

Why do American citizens hold elections to choose their government officials?

_____

_____

_____

_____

_____

_____

_____

_____

_____

_____

CHECK IN 1 2 3 4

A Plan for the People

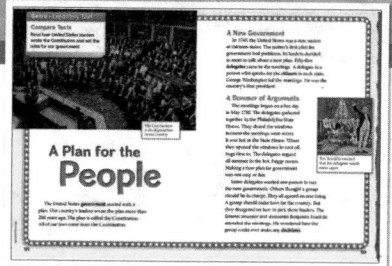

Literature Anthology:
pages 122–125

A Summer of Arguments

1   The meetings began on a hot day in May 1787. The delegates gathered together in the Philadelphia State House. They closed the windows because the meetings were secret. It was hot in the State House. When they opened the windows to cool off, bugs flew in. The delegates argued all summer in the hot, buggy rooms. Making a new plan for government was not easy or fun.

2   Some delegates wanted one person to run the new government. Others thought a group should be in charge. They all agreed on one thing. A group should make laws for the country. But they disagreed on how to pick these leaders. The famous inventor and statesman Benjamin Franklin attended the meetings. He wondered how the group could ever make any decisions.

Reread and use the prompts to take notes in the text.

Reread paragraph 1. **Underline** words that help you visualize what the Philadelphia State House was like during the meetings.

COLLABORATE

Talk with a partner about what the delegates agreed and disagreed about in paragraph 2. **Circle** the things they disagreed about.

Why is "A Summer of Arguments" a good heading for this section? Use your annotations to explain.

_____

_____

_____

_____

Making a Plan

3   The delegates wrote their plan and called it the United States Constitution. The Constitution was only a few pages long, but it was full of big ideas. The Constitution shows how our government works. It says that people are in charge of the government. People vote to pick their leaders. These leaders run the government for the people.

A Government That's Fair to All

4   The delegates planning the Constitution met for four months. They thought the Constitution was a good plan. But not all delegates signed it on September 15, 1787. Some of them wanted to make sure the government protected people's rights, too. A right is something you are allowed to have or do. In 1791, Congress changed the Constitution to protect the rights of American citizens. One right allows people to speak freely. These changes were called the Bill of Rights.

Underline the sentences in paragraph 3 that help you understand more about the Constitution.

COLLABORATE

Reread paragraph 4. Talk with a partner about how the author uses cause and effect to explain how the Bill of Rights was created. Remember to listen and respond to the information presented by your partner.

Circle why some delegates decided not to sign the Constitution.

What was the effect? **Draw a box around** it and write it here.

_____

_____

_____

_____

_____

_____

How does the author use headings to help you learn how America's leaders wrote the Constitution?

Talk About It Reread the headings on **Literature Anthology** pages 123 and 124. Talk with a partner about why the author uses these headings to organize the text.

Cite Text Evidence How does each heading help organize and explain the topic? Write text evidence in the web.

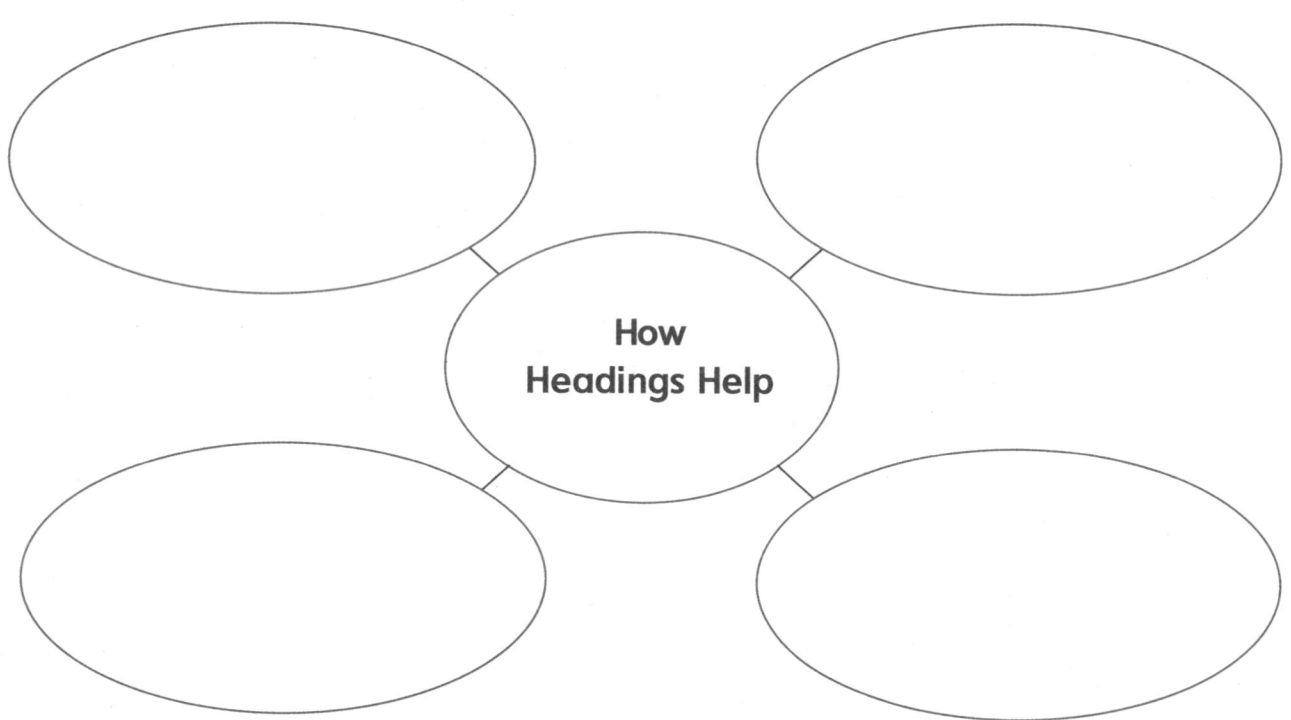

How Headings Help

Write The author uses headings to help me understand _____

CHECK IN 1 2 3 4

Author's Purpose

An author has a purpose, or reason, for writing. An author can write to inform, entertain, or persuade. Choosing the right text structure, or way to organize text, supports the author's purpose.

FIND TEXT EVIDENCE

In the last paragraph of page 140, the author uses a compare-and-contrast text structure to help readers understand the different sides of an important debate about our government.

> Some delegates wanted one person to run the new government. Others thought a group should be in charge. They all agreed on one thing. A group should make laws for the country. But they disagreed on how to pick these leaders.

Your Turn Reread paragraph 4 on page 141.

- How does the author use text structure to help you understand why we have a Bill of Rights? _____

_____

_____

_____

CHECK IN 1 > 2 > 3 > 4 >

How does the information you read in *Vote!* and "A Plan for the People" help you understand what is happening in the engraving?

Talk About It With a partner, discuss what you see in the engraving. Read the caption and talk about what happened to make the event shown in the engraving possible.

Cite Text Evidence Reread the caption. **Underline** evidence that explains how people make government work. **Circle** one clue in the engraving that shows that George Washington is taking the oath of office.

Write The information in "Vote!" and "A Plan for the People" helps me understand more about what is

happening in the engraving by _____

_____

_____

_____

_____

_____

_____

Time & Life Pictures/The LIFE Picture Collection/Getty Images

Quick Tip

George Washington is in the middle of the engraving. Seeing him there helps me compare text to art.

WASHINGTON TAKING THE OATH AS PRESIDENT,
APRIL 30, 1789, ON THE SITE OF THE PRESENT TREASURY BUILDING, WALL STREET, NEW YORK CITY.

This engraving shows George Washington taking the oath of office on April 30, 1789. Americans voted for Washington, and on this day he was sworn in as their president.

CHECK IN 1 2 3 4

Create a PSA

Think about what you learned from the texts you read about how people make government work. Why is voting an important part of government? Use text evidence to support your ideas.

1 Look at your Build Knowledge notes in your reader's notebook.

2 A public service announcement, or PSA, is a way to help people learn more about an issue. Plan a PSA that inspires people to vote. Your PSA could be a poster, pamphlet, or flyer. Think about how you can show people that voting is important.

3 Write the text of your PSA. Remember to cite evidence from the texts you read. Use new vocabulary words.

4 Add an illustration or photograph to your PSA to go along with what you wrote.

Think about what you learned in this text set. Fill in the bars on page 121.

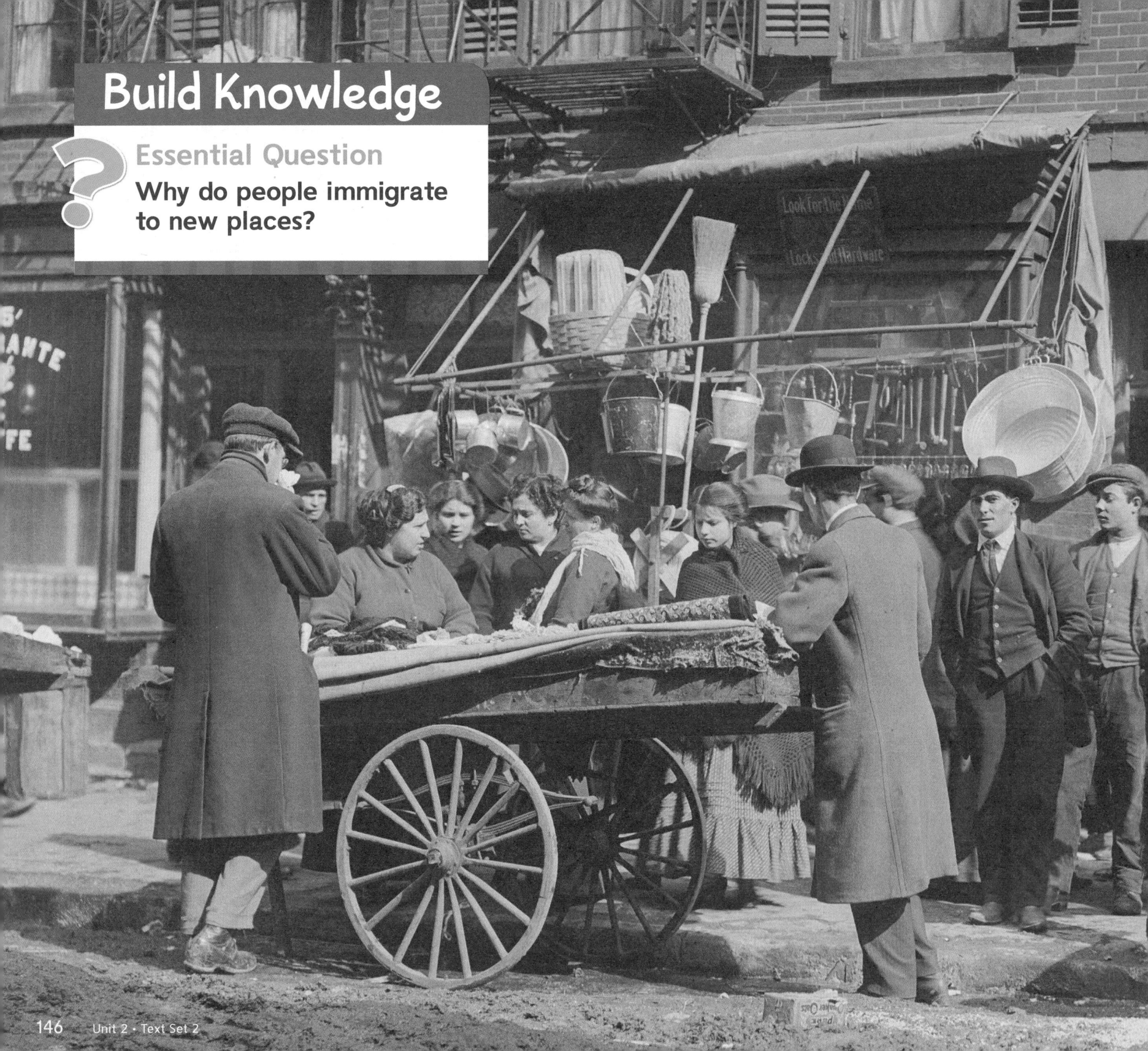

Build Knowledge

? **Essential Question**

Why do people immigrate to new places?

Build Vocabulary

Write new words you learned about immigration. Draw lines and circles for the words you write.

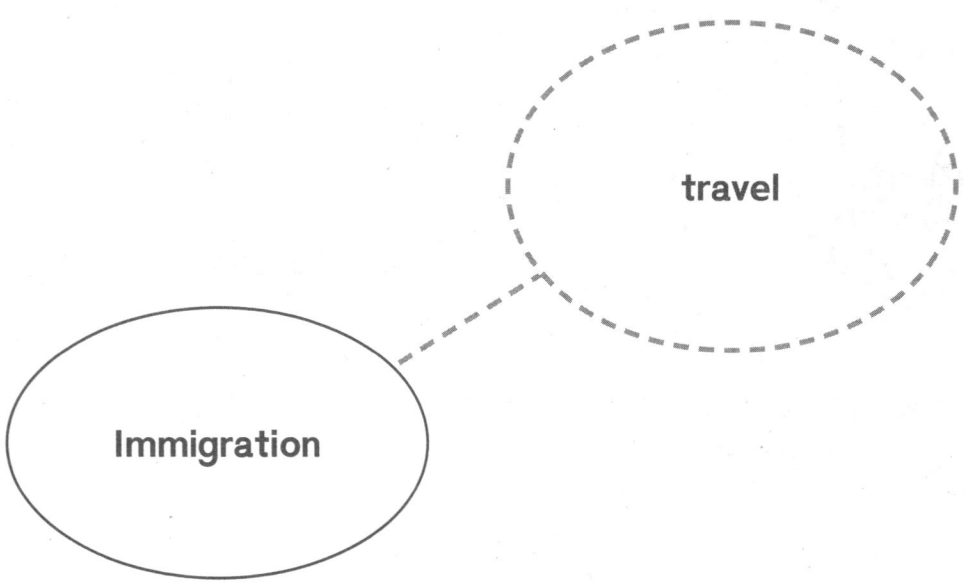

travel

Immigration

Go online to **my.mheducation.com** and read the "Leaving Home" Blast. Think about why learning about reasons for immigration is important. Then blast back your response.

Think about what you already know. Fill in the bars. There are no wrong answers here.

Key

1 = I do not understand.

2 = I understand but need more practice.

3 = I understand.

4 = I understand and can teach someone.

What I Know Now

I can read and understand historical fiction.

| 1 | 2 | 3 | 4 |

I can use text evidence to respond to historical fiction.

| 1 | 2 | 3 | 4 |

I know why people immigrate to new places.

| 1 | 2 | 3 | 4 |

STOP You will come back to the next page later.

Think about what you learned. Fill in the bars. What helped you the most?

What I Learned

I can read and understand historical fiction.

| 1 | 2 | 3 | 4 |

I can use text evidence to respond to historical fiction.

| 1 | 2 | 3 | 4 |

I know why people immigrate to new places.

| 1 | 2 | 3 | 4 |

SHARED READ

My Goal I can read and understand historical fiction.

TAKE NOTES

As you read, make note of interesting words and important events.

SAILING TO AMERICA

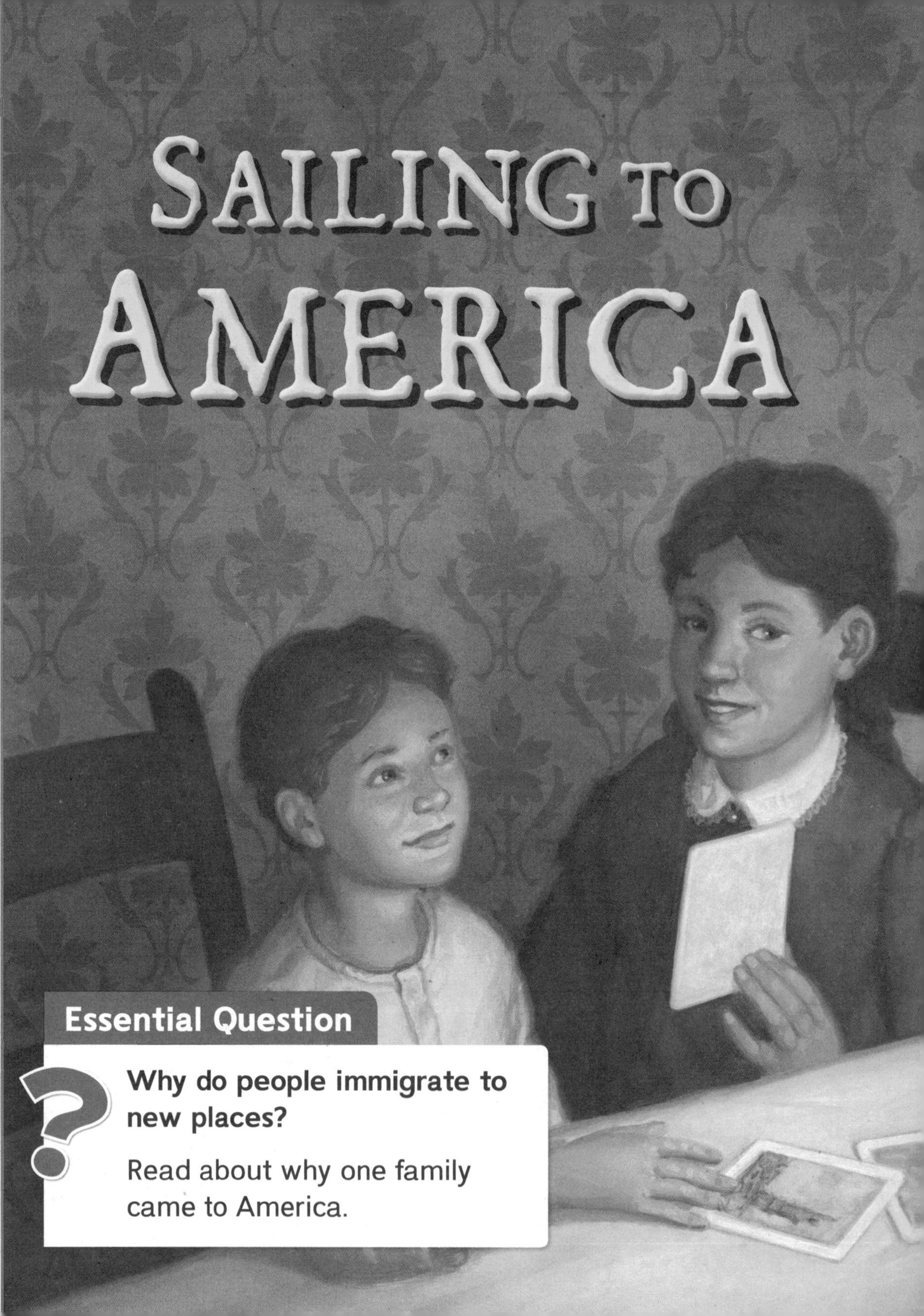

Essential Question

Why do people immigrate to new places?

Read about why one family came to America.

Nora woke early. She hadn't slept much. It was March, 1895. Da was leaving for America today. Uncle Sean **immigrated** there last year and found work right away. He asked Da to join him. It was Mama and Da's dream to one day live in America.

Nora lit a lamp for light and sat down at the table. Her brother, Danny, joined her.

"I feel like crying," he **whispered** softly.

"I know," Nora answered. "So do I, but this is Da and Mama's dream. Da will find work and send for us. Look at the **photographs** that Uncle Sean sent. Doesn't America look grand?"

FIND TEXT EVIDENCE

Read

Paragraph 1

Theme

What happened to Uncle Sean when he got to America?

_____

_____

Circle text evidence.

Paragraphs 2–4

Plot: Character Development

How do Nora and Danny feel about Da moving to America?

_____

_____

_____

Underline text evidence.

Reread

Author's Craft

How does the author help you understand that Nora and her family lived a long time ago?

FIND TEXT EVIDENCE

> Read

Paragraph 1
Theme
Circle two reasons Danny doesn't want to go to America.

Paragraphs 2–3
Make Predictions
Predict how Nora and Danny will feel when they arrive in America. Explain your answer.

_____

_____

_____

_____

Underline clues that helped you make your prediction.

> Reread

Author's Craft

How does the author use dialogue to help you understand how Danny and Nora feel about moving?

"I don't want to ever leave Ireland," Danny said. "We won't have any friends in America. We'll be far away from Grandda, Paddy, and Colleen."

"Maybe you'll be glad it isn't Ireland," Nora said. "There will be enough food to eat. Mama and Da can relax and not worry so much. We'll all have a better life. America will be the land of our dreams."

Then Da carried a bag into the room. "Cheer up, my little loves! Why, in no time at all, you'll be joining me."

A year later, Da had saved enough money to send for his family. Mama, Danny, and Nora packed what little they had. They got on a crowded steamship and began their voyage.

The trip across the Atlantic Ocean was rough. The air inside the steamship smelled like a dirty sock. The ship tossed up and down for days. The waves were as big as mountains. Many passengers became seasick, but Nora and Danny felt fine.

Every day Nora daydreamed and reread Da's letters. She thought of the buildings and streetcars he wrote about. In her dreams, she could picture Da on a crowded street. He had a big smile on his face.

FIND TEXT EVIDENCE

Read

Paragraphs 1–2
Theme
What was it like for passengers on the steamship?

_____

_____

_____

Circle text evidence.

Paragraph 3
Plot: Character Development
What does Nora do every day while she's on the steamship?

_____

_____

Underline text evidence.

Reread

Author's Craft

How does the illustration help you understand how Nora feels?

FIND TEXT EVIDENCE

Read

Paragraph 1
Make Predictions
What do you predict is happening as Nora wakes up?

_____

_____

Draw a box around clues.

Paragraph 2
Figurative Language
Underline text that compares two things. What is being compared?

_____

_____

Paragraph 3
Theme
Write how the people feel when they arrive in America.

_____

_____

Circle text evidence.

One morning, Nora awoke. A **moment** later, she realized something was different. The ocean was as smooth as glass.

A few hours later, Nora, Danny, and Mama shivered together on the ship's deck. Snowflakes drifted through the air. Another traveler noticed and gave them a blanket. It was as thin as a rag, but nothing could have been more **valuable** to them.

Suddenly, someone shouted, "There's Lady Liberty!" As the ship passed the large statue, the crowd cheered. Someone shouted, "At last, we've **arrived**! We are in America." Soon, everyone was singing and dancing.

A ferry took the travelers to Ellis Island. In the main hall, doctors **inspected** the family. They looked for signs of illness. Mama had to answer many questions. Nora knew that people didn't get an **opportunity**, or chance, to take these tests twice. Nora looked at Danny, then at Mama. They had to pass.

After a few hours, the family learned they could stay in America. As they filed off the ferry, Nora saw Uncle Sean's dark hair. Then she saw Da. His hands waved wildly. He had a big smile on his face. Dreams do come true, Nora thought as she waved back.

Summarize

Use your notes and think about what happens in "Sailing to America." Use the plot events to summarize the story.

HISTORICAL FICTION

FIND TEXT EVIDENCE

Read

Paragraph 1
Theme
What happens when Mama, Nora, and Danny get to Ellis Island?

_____

_____

Underline text evidence.

Paragraph 2
Plot: Character Development
What does Nora think and do when she sees Da?

_____

_____

Circle text evidence.

Reread

Author's Craft

How does the author help you understand how Nora feels at Ellis Island?

Vocabulary

Use the sentences to talk with a partner about each word. Then answer the questions.

arrived

I rang the doorbell when I **arrived** at my friend's house.

What do you do after you have arrived at school?

_____

_____

immigrated

Many people **immigrated** to the United States from other countries.

Why have some people immigrated to the United States?

_____

_____

inspected

Dad carefully **inspected** the tire to find out where the hole was.

What is something that you have inspected carefully?

_____

_____

moment

The bee landed on the flower for a **moment** and then flew away.

What can you do that lasts only a moment?

_____

opportunity

Our class had an **opportunity**, or chance, to visit the science museum.

What is another word for *opportunity*?

_____

 **Build Your Word List** Pick one of the interesting words you listed on page 150. Use a print or online dictionary to find the word's meaning. Then use the word in a sentence in your reader's notebook.

photographs

Looking at old **photographs** reminds me of things I've forgotten.

What can you learn from family photographs?

_____

_____

valuable

The card I made is very **valuable** to my grandmother.

Describe something that is valuable to you.

_____

_____

whispered

Kara **whispered** in Sofia's ear so no one else would hear her secret.

What is the opposite of *whispered*?

_____

_____

Figurative Language

Figurative language is words and phrases that hint at more than the words' literal meaning. Two kinds of figurative language are simile and hyperbole. A simile compares two things using *like* or *as*. Hyperbole is exaggeration.

FIND TEXT EVIDENCE

On page 152, "Why, in no time at all, you'll be joining me" is hyperbole. Da is exaggerating to cheer up Nora and Danny. On page 153, "The waves were as big as mountains" is a simile. This comparison makes the waves seem huge.

> Why, in no time at all, you'll be joining me.
>
> The waves were as big as mountains.

Your Turn Explain the meaning of *"The air inside the steamship smelled like a dirty sock"* from page 153. Is this a simile or hyperbole?

_____

_____

CHECK IN 〉 1 〉 2 〉 3 〉 4 〉

Make Predictions

Use story clues to predict what happens next. Was your prediction right? Reread to confirm, or check, it. Change it if it isn't right. Confirming predictions is a good way to check your understanding.

🔍 **FIND TEXT EVIDENCE**

What will Da do after he reaches America? You may have predicted that he would send for his family. Reread pages 152 and 153 for clues to support your prediction.

Quick Tip

A story's setting can give clues about what will happen next. You can use the change of setting from Ireland to America to predict what the characters in "Sailing to America" will do.

> **Page 152**
>
> "I don't want to ever leave Ireland," Danny said. "We won't have any friends in America. We'll be far away from Grandda, Paddy, and Colleen."
>
> "Maybe you'll be glad it isn't Ireland," Nora said. "There will be enough food to eat. Mama and Da can relax and not worry so much. We'll all have a better life. America will be the land of our dreams."
>
> Then Da carried a bag into the room. "Cheer up, my little loves! Why, in no time at all, you'll be joining me."

I predicted Da would bring his family to America. Here is the clue. Da says they will be joining him. I read page 153 to check my prediction. "A year later, Da had saved enough money to send for his family."

 **Your Turn** Predict what will happen when the family gets to America. Find clues to support your prediction.

_____

_____

CHECK IN 1 2 3 4

Plot: Character Development

"Sailing to America" is **historical fiction**. Historical fiction

- is a made-up story that takes place in the past
- has characters that develop from the beginning to the end

FIND TEXT EVIDENCE

I can tell that "Sailing to America" is historical fiction. The story is made up, but it is based on real events that happened a long time ago. Nora develops, or changes, throughout the story.

Page 151

Nora woke early. She hadn't slept much. It was March, 1895. Da was leaving for America today. Uncle Sean **immigrated** there last year and found work right away. He asked Da to join him. It was Mama and Da's dream to one day live in America.

Nora lit a lamp for light and sat down at the table. Her brother, Danny, joined her.

"I feel like crying," he **whispered** softly.

"I know," Nora answered. "So do I, but this is Da and Mama's dream. Da will find work and send for us. Look at the **photographs** that Uncle Sean sent. Doesn't America look grand?"

Readers to Writers

Notice the details the author uses in "Sailing to America" to help you know what the characters feel and think. When you write, think about specific details you can use to show your characters' feelings and thoughts.

Character Development

Characters change as a result of things they learn and experiences they have. To understand how a character changes, pay attention to what they say, how they feel, and what they do in different situations.

Your Turn How does Nora develop, or change, throughout "Sailing to America"? Use text evidence in your answer.

_____

_____

_____

CHECK IN ⟩ 1 ⟩ 2 ⟩ 3 ⟩ 4 ⟩

Theme

The theme of a story is the author's message. To figure out the theme, notice what the characters do and say. Think about what deeper ideas these important details suggest. These details can help you see how a theme develops, or grows, throughout a story.

🔍 FIND TEXT EVIDENCE

In "Sailing to America," Mama and Da dream of living in America. I think this is an important detail. I will reread to find more details. Then I can figure out the story's theme.

Detail
It's Mama and Da's dream to live in America.

↓

Detail
Danny is upset about leaving Ireland.

↓

Theme

Details tell what the characters do and say. They help you figure out the theme.

Your Turn Reread "Sailing to America." Find more important details and write them in the graphic organizer. Use the details above and the ones you wrote to figure out the theme.

CHECK IN ▷ 1 ▷ 2 ▷ 3 ▷ 4

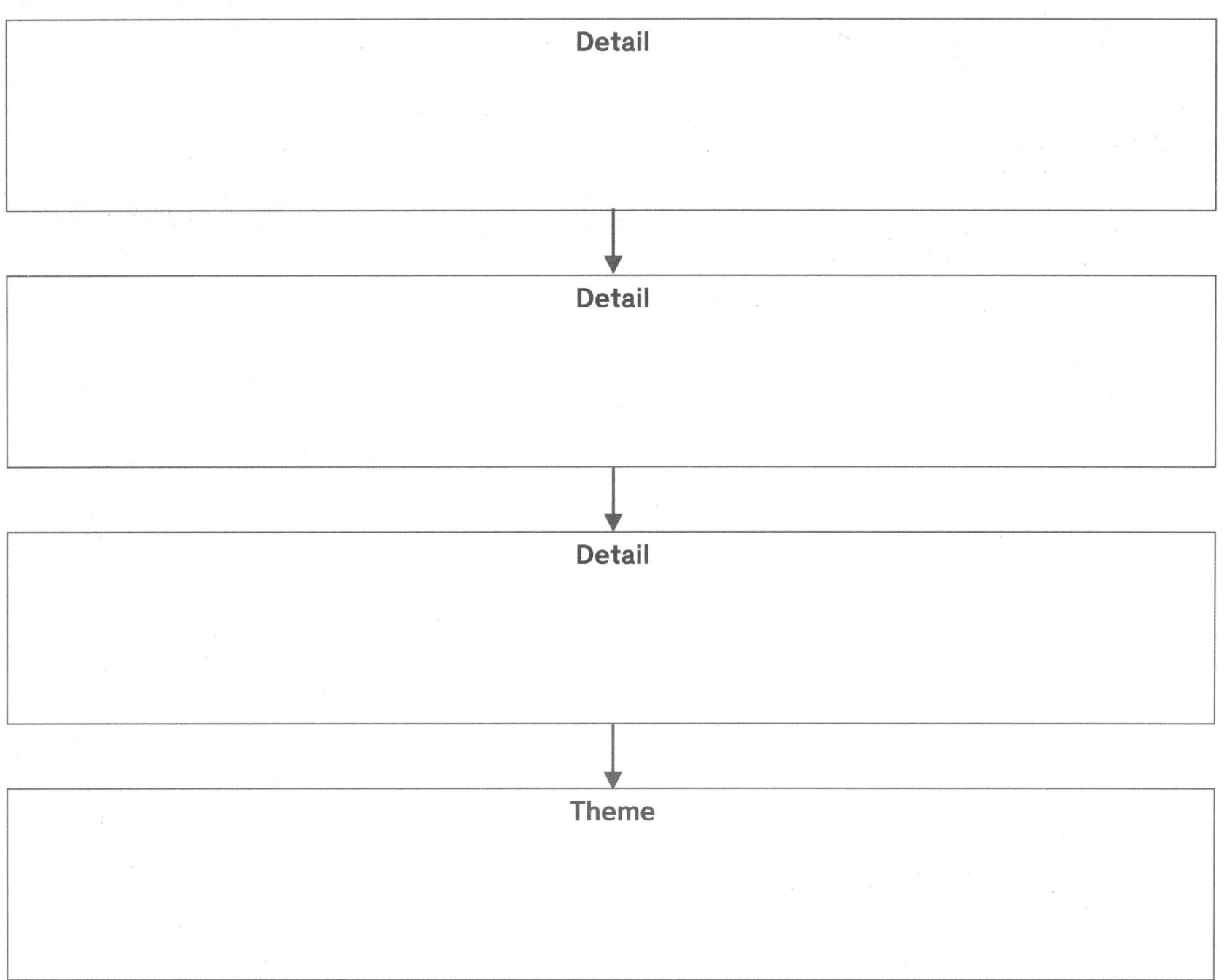

Detail

Detail

Detail

Theme

My Goal

I can use text evidence to respond to historical fiction.

Respond to Reading

Talk about the prompt below. Use your notes and evidence from the text to support your answer.

COLLABORATE

Do you think it was a good idea for Nora's family to immigrate to America? Why or why not?

_____

_____

_____

_____

_____

_____

_____

_____

_____

_____

_____

Quick Tip

Use these sentence starters to talk about immigration.

Immigrating to America was/was not a good idea because . . .

Life in America will be different because . . .

Grammar Connections

As you write your response, be sure to check that you have capitalized the names of people and places. Remember to use a punctuation mark at the end of each sentence.

CHECK IN 〉 1 〉 2 〉 3 〉 4

Immigration to the United States

Primary sources are sources by someone who experienced an event firsthand. They include photographs, letters, and journals. Secondary sources are created by someone who did not experience the event as it happened. They include encyclopedias, informative articles, and websites.

COLLABORATE

Write a journal entry from the perspective of someone immigrating to the United States in the 1800s. Work with a partner to gather information that will help you write your entry.

Step 1 **Set a Goal** Choose the country that the subject of your journal entry is moving from.

Step 2 **Identify Sources** Use primary and secondary sources to find information about the experiences of immigrants coming to the United States from the country you chose.

Step 3 **Find and Record Information** Take notes on what people traveling to the United States in the 1800s experienced. Why did some people decide to move to America at that time? Remember to cite your sources.

Step 4 **Organize and Combine Information** Organize your notes. Think about information you learned that you would like to include in your journal entry. Think of a name for the person the journal belongs to.

Step 5 **Create and Present** Write your journal entry. Be sure to mention why your subject is immigrating to the United States. Share your entry with your partner.

CHECK IN ⟩ 1 ⟩ 2 ⟩ 3 ⟩ 4 ⟩

The Castle on Hester Street

? **How does the author use dialogue to help you get to know what Julie's grandparents are like?**

Literature Anthology: pages 126–141

Talk About It Reread **Literature Anthology** page 130. Discuss with a partner how Julie's grandmother reacts to Sol's story.

Cite Text Evidence What clues in the dialogue help you get to know Julie's grandparents? Write text evidence in the diagram.

 Make Inferences

An inference is a conclusion based on facts and what you already know. What inference can you make about Julie's grandfather based on the story he tells Julie?

What Do the Characters Say?	What Does It Mean?

Write The author uses dialogue to _____

_____

_____

CHECK IN 1 2 3 4

How does the author show how Julie's grandmother and grandfather are different?

Talk About It Reread **Literature Anthology** page 132. Talk with a partner about Julie's grandmother's version of their journey.

Cite Text Evidence Now reread the last paragraph on page 133. What clues help you see how different Julie's grandparents are?

Julie's Grandmother	Julie's Grandfather	How They Are Different

Write I know Julie's grandparents are different because the author

_____

_____

CHECK IN 1 2 3 4

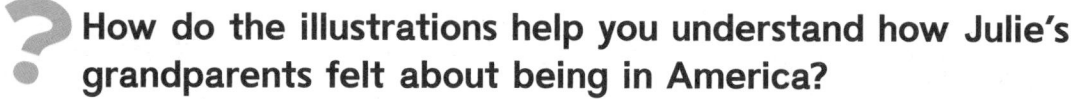

? **How do the illustrations help you understand how Julie's grandparents felt about being in America?**

Talk About It Look at the illustrations on **Literature Anthology** pages 135 and 136. Talk with a partner about what they show.

Cite Text Evidence What clues in the illustrations show how Julie's grandparents feel about being in America? Write clues in the chart.

How Do Julie's Grandparents Feel?	
Clues on page 135	Clues on page 136
What They Mean	What They Mean

Write The illustrations help me understand _____

_____

_____

Respond to Reading

COLLABORATE

Talk about the prompt below. Use your notes and evidence from the text to support your answer.

Why do you think Julie's grandparents tell different stories about coming to America?

_____

_____

_____

_____

_____

_____

_____

_____

_____

Quick Tip

Use these sentence starters to talk about Julie's grandparents.

Julie's grandfather's stories are . . .

Julie's grandmother's stories are . . .

Julie's grandparents tell different stories because . . .

CHECK IN   1 2 3 4

Next Stop, America!

*Literature Anthology:
pages 144–147*

What Happened at Ellis Island

1 Immigrants crossed the ocean on crowded ships. When the ships arrived in New York harbor, smaller boats took them to Ellis Island. There the travelers hoped to become American citizens. Thousands of people came every day.

2 First, everyone had to have a check-up. The government didn't want sick people coming into the country. As a result, some sick people stayed in the Ellis Island hospital until they were well. Someone with an eye infection was sent back across the ocean!

3 People also had to take a written test. They had to answer questions, give their names, and tell what country they were from. They had to tell where they planned to go. They had to promise to obey the laws of the United States.

4 After hours of waiting, most people got good news. The United States welcomed them to their new home.

Reread and use the prompts to take notes in the text.

In paragraph 1, **circle** how many people came to Ellis Island every day.

Reread paragraphs 2 and 3. **Write numbers next to** sentences that describe what immigrants had to do at Ellis Island.

COLLABORATE

Reread paragraph 4. Talk with a partner about how immigrants felt about being allowed to stay in America. How many got to stay? **Underline** text that answers the question. Write it here.

_____

_____

_____

Where They Went

5   From Ellis Island, some immigrants got on ferries to New York City. Many people's journeys ended there. Thousands settled near friends and family. They stayed in neighborhoods, such as Little Italy and the Lower East Side. Others had more traveling to do. They headed west or south, to other cities and states. Some went to places where they could get a job in a factory or a mine. Others found good farmland. No matter where the immigrants settled, they never forgot Ellis Island.

Reread paragraph 5. **Underline** the sentence that helps you understand that most of the immigrants stayed in New York. Write it here.

_____

_____

Circle places where immigrants settled.

COLLABORATE

Talk with a partner about why Ellis Island was a memorable place for immigrants.

Draw a box around the text evidence that supports your discussion.

Bettmann/Getty Images

? **How do the headings help you understand what it was like to immigrate to America?**

Talk About It Reread the excerpts on pages 168 and 169. Talk about why "What Happened at Ellis Island" is a good heading.

Cite Text Evidence What clues in the headings and photograph help you understand the text better? Write them in the chart.

Quick Tip

Clue	Clue	Clue

↓ ↓ ↓

How It Helps

Write The author uses headings to _____

_____

_____

CHECK IN 1 2 3 4

Bettmann/Getty Images

Cause and Effect

A cause is why something happens. An effect is what happens. Cause and effect happen in time order. Words such as *because* and *as a result* signal cause and effect.

FIND TEXT EVIDENCE

*On page 145 of "Next Stop, America!" in the **Literature Anthology**, I read that many immigrants came to America. This is the effect. I can use the signal word* because *to find the cause. Immigrants wanted the right to live and speak as they wished. That's why they came.*

> They came to America because they wanted the right to live and speak as they wished.

Your Turn Reread the second paragraph on page 168.

- How does the author help you figure out what the effect is?

_____

_____

- How do you know what the cause is?_____

_____

CHECK IN 1 2 3 4

? How do the *The Castle on Hester Street,* "Next Stop, America!," and the photograph below help you understand why people came to America?

  **Talk About It** Read the caption and look at the photograph. Talk with a partner about what you notice. Choose one person in the photo and describe what he is doing.

Cite Text Evidence **Circle** three clues in the photograph that help you understand what the boys are doing. **Underline** words and phrases in the caption that give more information about why immigrants come to America.

Write The photograph, *The Castle on Hester Street,* and "Next Stop, America!" help me understand that people came to America to

_____

_____

_____

_____

_____

Library of Congress Prints and Photographs Division [LC-DIG-nclc-04549]

> **Quick Tip**
>
> The photograph helps me understand how hard immigrants had to work. This helps me compare the texts with the photograph.

This photograph was taken in 1909 by photographer Lewis Wickes Hine. It is called "Immigrants in Night School" and shows a classroom in Boston, Massachusetts.

CHECK IN 1 2 3 4

My Goal I know why people immigrate to new places.

Design a Museum Brochure

Think over what you learned about why people immigrate to new places. Why do you think it's important to learn about immigrants' stories? Use text evidence to support your ideas.

1. Look at your Build Knowledge notes in your reader's notebook.

2. Create a brochure for visitors to an immigration museum. Describe some of the museum's exhibits.

3. Add a paragraph to your brochure about why it's important to learn about immigrants' stories. Use examples from the texts you read. Use new vocabulary words in your writing.

4. Add some illustrations to your brochure to represent what visitors might see in the museum.

Think about what you learned in this text set. Fill in the bars on page 149.

Build Knowledge

Essential Question

How do people figure things out?

Build Vocabulary

 Write new words you learned about how people figure things out. Draw lines and circles for the words you write.

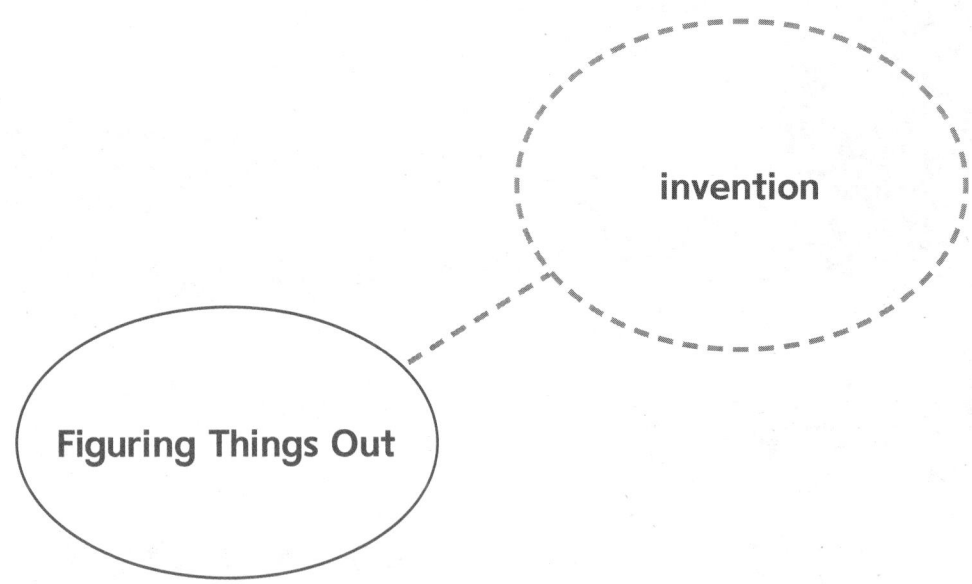

invention

Figuring Things Out

 Go online to **my.mheducation.com** and read the "I Spy with My Little Eye" Blast. Think about why learning about how scientists answer questions is important. Then blast back your response.

MY GOALS

Think about what you already know. Fill in the bars. You'll keep learning more.

Key

1 =	I do not understand.
2 =	I understand but need more practice.
3 =	I understand.
4 =	I understand and can teach someone.

What I Know Now

I can read and understand poetry.

> 1 > 2 > 3 > 4 >

I can use text evidence to respond to poetry.

> 1 > 2 > 3 > 4 >

I know how people figure things out.

> 1 > 2 > 3 > 4 >

STOP You will come back to the next page later.

Think about what you learned. Fill in the bars. Keep up the good work!

What I Learned

I can read and understand poetry.

1 2 3 4

I can use text evidence to respond to poetry.

1 2 3 4

I know how people figure things out.

1 2 3 4

My Goal I can read and understand poetry.

TAKE NOTES

As you read, make note of interesting words and details.

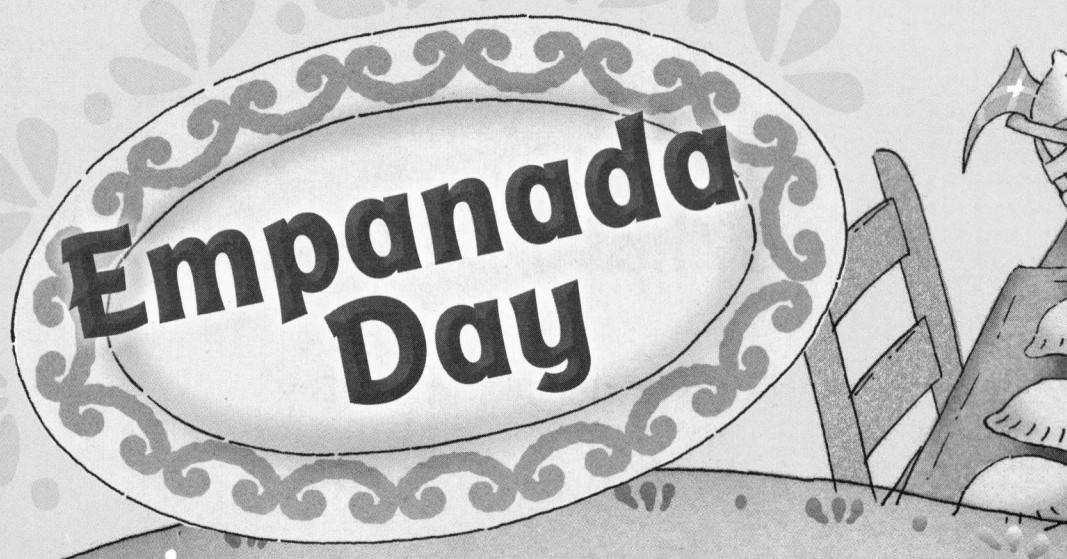

Empanada Day

One bite of Abuelita's empanadas
And my mouth purrs like a cat.
  "Teach me," I beg and bounce on my feet,
  "Teach me to make this magical treat."
Abuelita smiles,
  "Be an observer, watch and learn,
  Then you too can take a turn."

Essential Question

How do people figure things out?

Read poems about different ways to figure things out.

She sets before me a ball of dough,
Round and golden as the sun.
My eyes wide as saucers, I watch and follow,

Press circles flat as pancakes,
Spoon on apple slices and nose-tickling spices,
Seal it all in, a half-moon envelope of bliss.
Together we write down every step
As the empanadas bake and crisp in the oven,
My stomach rumbling like a hungry bear.
Ah, empanada day!

— George Santiago

POETRY

FIND TEXT EVIDENCE

Read
Page 178
Alliteration
Underline words in the last line that start with the same sound.

Page 179
Figurative Language
A simile uses the word *like* or *as* to compare two different things. **Circle** the similes. Pick one and write what it compares.

_____

_____

Pages 178–179
Character Perspective
Who is the speaker, or narrator, of this poem?

_____

Reread
Author's Craft

How does the poet help you understand how empanadas are made?

FIND TEXT EVIDENCE 🔍

Read

Page 180

Rhymed Verse

Underline three words that rhyme in "Cold Feet."

Alliteration

Draw a box around two words that start with the same sound in "Our Washing Machine."

Character Perspective

What does the speaker think about the washing machine?

_____

_____

_____

Circle text evidence.

Reread

Author's Craft

In "Cold Feet," how does the poet help you visualize the inventor's problem?

Cold Feet

An inventor with feet like ice,

And toes like ten shivering mice,

Looked at clothes, studied feet.

Read about cold and heat,

And knit the first socks, warm and nice.

OUR WASHING MACHINE

Our washing machine is a bear

That munches up socks by the pair.

He will suds them and grumble

As they spin, turn, and tumble,

Then spit them out, ready to wear.

Bugged

A creature has crawled on my knee,

It's a bug green and round as a pea.

His five wings are fish fins,

He's got teeth sharp as pins.

Just imagine him chomping on me!

I read every bug book I see,

To learn what this creature might be.

I ask scientists too,

But they don't have a clue.

So I'm **bugged** by this great mystery.

Make Connections

What do all four poems have in common? Use your notes to talk about how they are alike.

FIND TEXT EVIDENCE

Read

Page 181

Character Perspective

How does the speaker feel about the creature?

_____

_____

_____

Underline text evidence.

Rhymed Verse

Circle three words that rhyme. Then find two more words that rhyme. Write them here.

_____

_____

Reread

Author's Craft

Why is "Bugged" a good title for this poem?

Vocabulary

Use the sentences to talk with a partner about each word. Then answer the questions.

bounce

Keith likes to **bounce** a soccer ball off his head.

How many times can you bounce a ball?

_____

_____

imagine

Mandy likes to **imagine** what it was like to live 100 years ago.

What do you like to imagine?

_____

_____

inventor

Thomas Edison is the **inventor** of the first light bulb.

What does an inventor do?

_____

_____

observer

Gina is a good **observer** and enjoys watching birds.

Write about a time when you were an observer at an event.

_____

_____

Poetry Words

alliteration

"Poets paint pretty pictures" is an example of **alliteration**.

Give another example of alliteration.

_____

_____

free verse

Jeremy likes to write **free verse** because it doesn't need to rhyme.

What would you write a free-verse poem about?

_____

_____

limerick

Hana's **limerick** had five lines and made the class laugh.

How is a limerick different from other poems?

_____

_____

rhyme

The words _cat_ and _bat_ **rhyme** because they end in the same sound.

Name two other words that rhyme.

_____

_____

> **Build Your Word List**
> Underline the word _rumbling_ on page 179 of "Empanada Day." Draw a word web in your reader's notebook. Write the word _rumbling_ in the center. Then use a dictionary to fill in other forms of the word.

Figurative Language

Figurative language is words and phrases that mean something different than the words' literal meaning. Two kinds of figurative language are simile and metaphor. A simile is a comparison using _like_ or _as_. A metaphor is a comparison that doesn't use _like_ or _as_.

🔍 FIND TEXT EVIDENCE

In "Cold Feet," the phrase "feet like ice" is a simile that shows how cold the speaker's feet are. In "Our Washing Machine," the line "our washing machine is a bear" is a metaphor that helps the reader picture the washing machine.

> An inventor with feet like ice,
>
> Our washing machine is a bear

Your Turn Reread "Cold Feet." Find an example of figurative language and write it below. Is it a simile or a metaphor? What does it mean?

_____

_____

CHECK IN 1 2 3 4

Alliteration and Rhymed Verse

Poets use alliteration and rhyme to draw attention to certain words and to make poems sound musical.

Alliteration is the use of words that start with the same sound. **Rhyme** is when words end in the same sound.

FIND TEXT EVIDENCE

Read aloud the poem "Bugged" on page 181. Listen for beginning sounds that repeat. Listen for words that rhyme.

Page 181

Bugged

A creature has crawled on my knee,
It's a bug green and round as a pea.
His five wings are fish fins,
He's got teeth sharp as pins.
Just imagine him chomping on me!

I read every bug book I see,
To learn what this creature might be.
I ask scientists too,
But they don't have a clue.
So I'm **bugged** by this great mystery.

In the first line, the words creature *and* crawled *start with the same sound.*

The words knee *and* pea *rhyme. I like the way these words sound.*

COLLABORATE

Your Turn Reread "Bugged." Write two more examples of alliteration here.

_____

_____

CHECK IN 1 2 3 4

Limerick and Free Verse

A **limerick** is a kind of rhymed verse. It is a short, funny poem that rhymes. Each stanza has five lines. The first, second, and fifth lines rhyme. The third and fourth lines rhyme. This pattern of rhyme is called the poem's rhyme scheme.

Free verse does not always rhyme. It can have any number of lines and stanzas.

FIND TEXT EVIDENCE

I can tell that "Cold Feet" is a limerick. It is funny. The stanza has five lines. Some of the lines rhyme.

Page 180

Cold Feet

An inventor with feet like ice,
And toes like ten shivering mice,
Looked at clothes, studied feet.
Read about cold and heat,
And knit the first socks, warm and nice.

OUR WASHING MACHINE

Our washing machine is a bear
That munches up socks by the pair.
He will suds them and grumble
As they spin, turn, and tumble,
Then spit them out, ready to wear.

In this funny limerick, the first, second, and fifth lines rhyme. This limerick has one stanza. A stanza is a group of lines in a poem.

COLLABORATE

Your Turn Reread the poems "Our Washing Machine" and "Empanada Day." Explain whether each poem is free verse or a limerick. Write your answer below.

_____

_____

_____

CHECK IN 1 2 3 4

Character Perspective

A poem often shows the perspective of the poem's speaker, or narrator. To understand the speaker's perspective, look for details that show his or her thoughts and feelings.

🔍 FIND TEXT EVIDENCE

I'll read "Empanada Day" and look for details that show what the speaker thinks about making empanadas with Abuelita, his grandmother. This is his perspective.

Details
One bite of Abuelita's empanadas and my mouth purrs like a cat.
Teach me to make this magical treat.
My eyes wide as saucers, I watch and follow.

↓

Perspective

Your Turn Reread "Empanada Day." Write more details and the speaker's perspective in the graphic organizer. Use what you learned to discuss perspective in another poem.

CHECK IN   1 ⟩ 2 ⟩ 3 ⟩ 4 ⟩

Details

↓

Perspective

My Goal I can use text evidence to respond to poetry.

Respond to Reading

COLLABORATE Talk about the prompt below. Use your notes and evidence from the text to support your answer.

Which poem helps you understand how people figure things out?

_____

_____

_____

_____

_____

_____

_____

_____

_____

_____

_____

Quick Tip

Use these sentence starters to talk about the prompt.

The poem that helps me understand how people figure things out is . . .

This is because . . .

Grammar Connections

As you write your response, make sure to place quotation marks around the title of the poem and any words you copy directly from the poem.

CHECK IN 1 2 3 4

Famous Inventors

An interview is a formal conversation between two people. It's a great way to gather information about a person or topic. Follow the research process to find answers to questions you could ask in an interview with a famous inventor. Work with a partner.

Step 1 **Set a Goal** Brainstorm a list of famous inventors with your partner. Choose one from your list to interview.

Step 2 **Identify Sources** Use encyclopedias, reliable websites, and videos to find information about the inventor you chose to interview.

Step 3 **Find and Record Information** Use your sources to gather information about the life of your inventor. Note what your inventor created and why.

Step 4 **Organize and Combine Information** Generate, or think of, three questions to ask your inventor. Organize your notes by sorting information into categories that answer each question.

Step 5 **Create and Present** Use your notes to write answers to each question from the perspective of your inventor. Practice reading through your interview with your partner. Then present your interview to the class.

Quick Tip

To write an interview, write the name of the person speaking, a colon, and then what the person says:

Julia: What did you invent?

Mary Anderson: I invented windshield wipers in 1903!

CHECK IN 1 2 3 4

The Inventor Thinks Up Helicopters

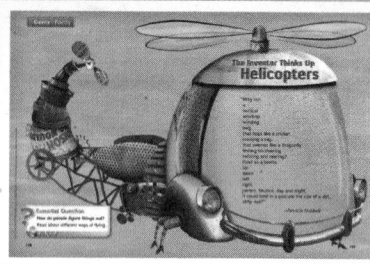

Literature Anthology: pages 148–149

? **How does the poet's use of alliteration help you visualize a helicopter?**

Talk About It Reread **Literature Anthology** page 149. Talk with a partner about how the poet's word choice affects the feel of the poem.

Cite Text Evidence How does alliteration help you picture a helicopter? Write text evidence in the chart.

Alliteration	I Visualize

Write The poet's use of alliteration helps me _____

_____

Combine Information

Reread "The Inventor Thinks Up Helicopters." Think about the questions the speaker asks. How do they help you understand her perspective?

CHECK IN 1 2 3 4

Ornithopter

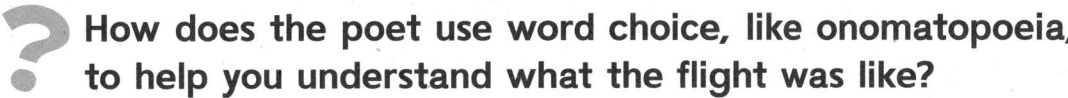

How does the poet use word choice, like onomatopoeia, to help you understand what the flight was like?

Talk About It Reread **Literature Anthology** page 150. With a partner, discuss if the poem is a limerick or free-verse poem. Talk about how the poet describes the sounds of the flight.

Cite Text Evidence What words and phrases describe sounds? Write text evidence in the word web.

Quick Tip

Onomatopoeia is the use of a word whose sound suggests its meaning. The word *purr* is onomatopoeia. It means "a soft, murmuring sound." When you say the word *purr* out loud, it sounds like what it means.

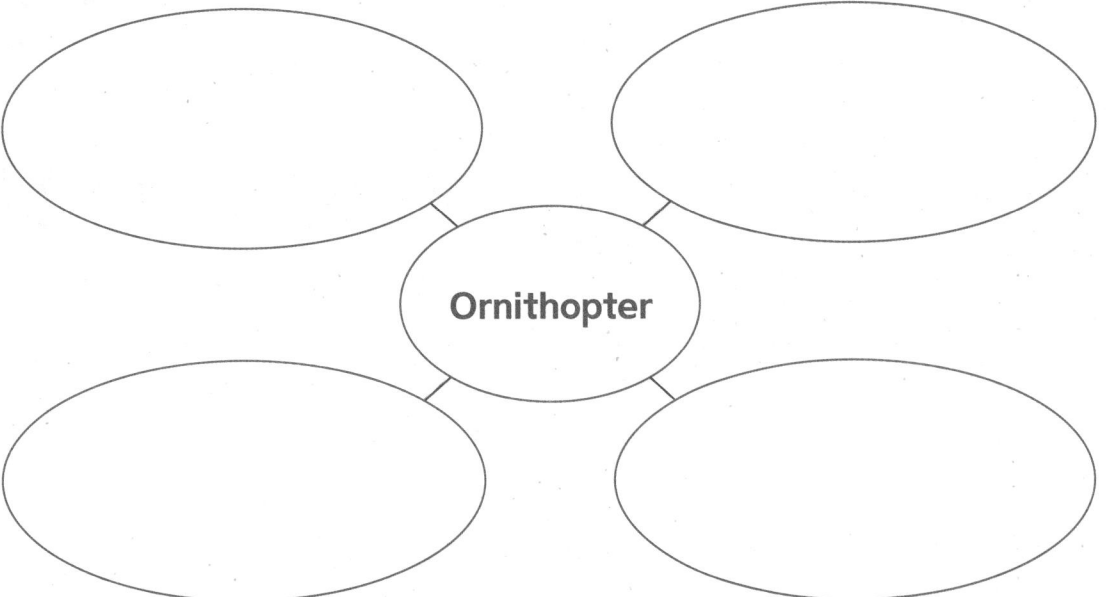

Ornithopter

Write I understand what it was like to be at the flight because

_____

_____

CHECK IN 1 2 3 4

Respond to Reading

COLLABORATE

Talk about the prompt below. Use your notes and evidence from the text to support your answer.

How do the poems help you understand how people invent things?

_____

_____

_____

_____

_____

_____

_____

_____

_____

Quick Tip

Use these sentence starters to talk about the poems.

"The Inventor Thinks Up Helicopters" helps me understand how people invent things by . . .

"Ornithopter" helps me understand that by . . .

CHECK IN 〉 1 〉 2 〉 3 〉 4

Montgolfier Brothers' Hot Air Balloon

Literature Anthology: pages 152–153

 **How does the poet use the illustration to set the mood for the poem?**

Talk About It Look at the illustration on **Literature Anthology** page 152. Talk about how the illustration adds meaning to the poem by setting the mood.

Cite Text Evidence What clues in the illustration help you get a feel for the poem? Write them in the chart.

 Make Inferences

Look at colors, details, and facial expressions in illustrations to make an inference about the poem's mood.

Clues	Mood

Write The author uses the illustration to set the mood by _____

_____

_____

CHECK IN ⟩ 1 ⟩ 2 ⟩ 3 ⟩ 4 ⟩

How does the poet's use of rhyme help you visualize the details of the hot air balloon's flight?

Talk About It Reread the poem on **Literature Anthology** page 153. Talk with a partner about the words that rhyme and how they help you picture the flight.

Cite Text Evidence What rhyming words help you visualize the balloon's flight? Find text evidence and write what you picture.

Montgolfier Brothers' Hot Air Balloon	
Words	**I Visualize**

Write The poet uses rhyme to help me visualize _____

_____

CHECK IN 1 2 3 4

Rhyme Scheme

Authors of rhymed verse often use a set rhyming pattern in their poems. This is called a rhyme scheme. To identify a poem's rhyme scheme, you can use letters to represent the different rhyming sounds at the end of each line in a poem.

FIND TEXT EVIDENCE

Reread the first stanza of "Montgolfier Brothers' Hot Air Balloon" on page 153 of the **Literature Anthology**. The letter *A* can stand for the final sound in *burner* in the first line. *B* can stand for the final sound in *furiously* in the second line. *C* can stand for the final sound in *rise* in the third line. In the fourth line, *aerially* rhymes with *furiously*. This means the rhyme scheme is *ABCB*.

Your Turn Reread the first stanza of "Ornithopter" on page 150 of the **Literature Anthology**. The rhyme scheme is *AABBA*. Which lines are represented by the letter *B*? Why do they share this letter?

_____

_____

_____

Readers to Writers

Here's an example of a poem with a rhyme scheme of *AABA*:

Blooming trees (A)
A gentle breeze (A)
Beautiful flowers (B)
And buzzing bees (A)

When you write your own rhymed verse, think how you can use different rhyme schemes.

CHECK IN 1 2 3 4

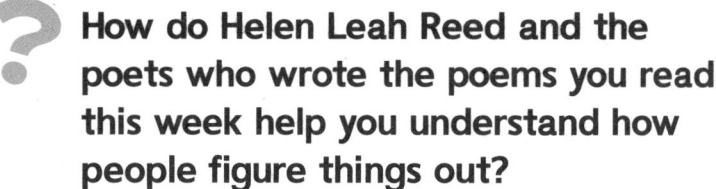

? **How do Helen Leah Reed and the poets who wrote the poems you read this week help you understand how people figure things out?**

Talk About It Read "A Curiosity." Talk with a partner about how the boy figures things out.

Cite Text Evidence Circle words and phrases in the poem that show the boy is curious. Review the poems you read this week and discuss ways the poets help you understand how people invent things.

Write Helen Leah Reed and the poets help me understand that people figure things out by

_____

_____

_____

_____

_____

_____

_____

"A Curiosity"

I knew a little boy, not very long ago,

Who was as bright and happy
    as any boy you know.

He had an only fault,
    and you will all agree

That from a fault like this a boy
    himself might free.

"I wonder who is there, oh, see!
    now, why is this?"

And "Oh, where are they going?"
    and "Tell me what it is?"

Ah! "which" and "why"
    and "who," and "what"
    and "where" and "when,"

We often wished that
    never need we
    hear those words again.

— Helen Leah Reed

Wavebreak Media ltd/Alamy Stock Photo; Reed, Helen Leah. *Memorial Day: And Other Verse* (original and Translated). Boston: De Wolfe and Fiske Company. 1917.

CHECK IN 1 2 3 4

Draw an Invention Diagram

Think over what you learned about how people figure things out. How can observing the world around you help you create something new? Use text evidence to support your ideas.

1. Look at your Build Knowledge notes in your reader's notebook.

2. Think of an invention of your own. Describe your invention's purpose and tell how it would work.

3. Draw a diagram of your invention. Include labels for its different parts.

4. Beneath your diagram, write a short paragraph that explains how observing people and things around us can help us create new things. Remember to use examples from the texts you read. Use new vocabulary words that you have learned.

Think about what you learned in this text set. Fill in the bars on page 177.

Think about what you already know. Fill in the bars. Meeting your goals may take time.

Key
1 = I do not understand.
2 = I understand but need more practice.
3 = I understand.
4 = I understand and can teach someone.

What I Know Now

I can write a realistic fiction story.

| 1 | 2 | 3 | 4 |

I can write a free-verse poem.

| 1 | 2 | 3 | 4 |

STOP You will come back to the next page later.

Think about what you learned. Fill in the bars. What do you want to work on more?

What I Learned

I can write a realistic fiction story.

1 2 3 4

I can write a free-verse poem.

1 2 3 4

Expert Model

Features of Realistic Fiction

Realistic fiction is a kind of narrative writing. A realistic fiction story

- is a made-up story that could really happen
- has a plot with a beginning, middle, and end and a logical sequence of events
- has dialogue, description, and illustrations

*Literature Anthology:
pages 26–43*

Analyze an Expert Model A good way to learn how to write a realistic fiction story is to read one. Reread the first two paragraphs on page 27 of *Yoon and the Jade Bracelet* in the **Literature Anthology**. Use text evidence to answer the questions.

How do you know this is realistic fiction?

_____

_____

How does the author help you understand how Yoon feels at the beginning of the story?

_____

_____

_____

Word Wise

On page 27, Helen Recorvits tells about what is happening to Yoon. This helps us understand how she feels. Gabi Swiatkowska's illustration helps us see how Yoon feels, too.

Plan: Choose Your Topic

COLLABORATE

Mapping With a partner, think of one or more characters you have read about who speak up for what they believe. When you write a realistic fiction story, your character should have talents or skills that real people have. Use the sentence starters below to discuss your ideas.

I read about a character who . . .

This character said . . .

He/she solved a problem by . . .

Writing Prompt Choose from your ideas to write a realistic fiction story about a character who speaks to a government leader.

I will write about _____

Purpose and Audience An author's purpose is the author's main reason for writing. Your audience is who will be reading it.

What is your purpose for writing your story? _____

_____

Who will read your realistic fiction story? _____

_____

Plan In your writer's notebook, make a Sequence of Events chart to plan your writing. Fill in the characters, setting, and the first event, or how you want the story to start.

Quick Tip

Mapping is a way to plan your writing. It can help you figure out the setting and plot of a story. It can also help you create realistic characters. Use a Sequence of Events chart to write down your ideas. Then use your ideas to write your story.

Character
Setting
Beginning
↓
Middle
↓
End

CHECK IN 1 ⟩ 2 ⟩ 3 ⟩ 4

Plan: Sequence of Events

Sequence of Events Writers tell a story's events in a logical order. These events make up the story's plot. Characters often have a problem in the beginning of a story that they solve by the end.

In "The Dream Catcher," Peter solves a problem. Reread to see how the author tells the sequence of events that lead to Peter's solution.

> Nokomis and Peter worked together and made a dream catcher. That night, as he gazed and looked at the dream catcher over his bed, he made a plan.
>
> The next morning he told Nokomis his plan. "I'm going to show my class how to make a dream catcher," he said.

How does the author help you see how Peter solves his problem?

_____

_____

Now think about your character. What is your character's problem? How will your character solve it?

_____

_____

Chart In your writer's notebook, complete your Sequence of Events chart with the remaining events in your story.

Quick Tip

Transitional words and phrases help the reader understand the sequence of events. Examples of transitional words and phrases include *first, then, next, later, that night,* and *the next day.*

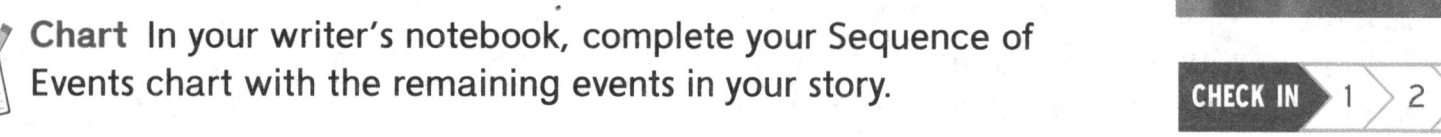

CHECK IN 1 2 3 4

Ken Karp/McGraw-Hill Education

Draft

Dialogue Dialogue is the actual words that characters in a story say to each other. Dialogue can show a character's response to a situation, their feelings and emotions, or their thoughts about events in the story. Reread this excerpt from *Yoon and the Jade Bracelet*. Pay attention to how the author uses dialogue to show how the characters feel.

> The next morning I waited in the school yard for the older girl.
>
> She was still wearing my jade bracelet.
>
> "It is time to give back my bracelet," I said.
>
> "I will give it to you later," she said, rushing past me.
>
> All morning my heart was heavy with worry.

Now use the above dialogue as a model to write what your characters might say to each other.

_____

_____

_____

Write a Draft Look over your Sequence of Events chart. Use it to help you write your draft in your writer's notebook. Remember to put story events in order and to include dialogue.

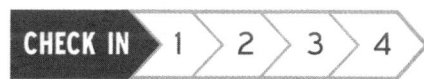

CHECK IN 1 2 3 4

Revise

Strong Conclusion Writers end a realistic fiction story with a satisfying conclusion. The conclusion should give a sense of closure, or a feeling that everything is settled. Readers should feel they've read all that happens and understand the story's theme.

Reread page 45 of "The Dream Catcher." Talk with a partner about how the author ends the story with a strong conclusion. Write about it here.

_____

_____

_____

Revise It's time to revise your writing. Read your draft and look for places where you might

- add dialogue and descriptive details

- make your conclusion stronger

Circle two sentences in your draft that you can change. Revise and write them here.

1 _____

2 _____

_____

CHECK IN 1 2 3 4

Peer Conferences

Review a Draft Listen carefully as a partner reads his or her draft aloud. Tell what you like about the draft. Use these sentence starters to help you discuss your partner's draft.

I like this part because . . .

Add more dialogue or description here to explain . . .

Add to your conclusion to show . . .

I have a question about . . .

Partner Feedback After you take turns giving each other feedback, write one of the suggestions from your partner that you will use in your revision.

_____

_____

_____

_____

_____

Revision After you finish your peer conference, use the Revising Checklist to help you figure out what you can change to make your realistic fiction story better. Remember to use the rubric on page 207 to help you with your revision.

Edit and Proofread

After you revise your realistic fiction story, proofread it to find any mistakes in grammar, spelling, and punctuation. Read your draft at least three times. This will help you catch any mistakes. Use the checklist below to edit your sentences.

✓ Editing Checklist

☐ Do all sentences begin with a capital letter and end with a punctuation mark?

☐ Are linking verbs used when appropriate?

☐ Are quotation marks used correctly in dialogue?

☐ Are all words spelled correctly?

Grammar Connections

When you proofread your draft for mistakes, remember to look for places where linking words, such as *am, is, was,* or *were,* can be used to connect subjects with more information that describes that subject. For example, "In class, she *was* very quiet, but on stage, she *was* loud and outgoing."

List two mistakes that you found as you proofread your realistic fiction story.

1 _____

_____

_____

2 _____

_____

_____

Publish, Present, and Evaluate

Publishing When you publish your writing, you create a neat final copy that is free of mistakes. Be sure to print neatly. Leave the space of a pencil point between letters and the space of the width of a pencil between words.

Presentation When you are ready to present, practice your presentation. Use the Presenting Checklist.

Evaluate After you publish, use the rubric to evaluate your writing.

Which parts of your story are you proud of? _____

_____

What might need more work? _____

_____

✓ **Presenting Checklist**

☐ Look at the audience.

☐ Speak slowly and carefully.

☐ Use expression when reading dialogue between characters.

☐ Show all illustrations to the audience.

> Turn to page 199. Fill in the bars to show what you learned.

4	3	2	1
• all events are in a logical order • dialogue and illustrations are used throughout the story • the story has a strong and satisfying conclusion	• most events are in a logical order • dialogue and illustrations are used in most of the story • the story has a strong and mostly satisfying conclusion	• some events are out of order • dialogue and illustrations are used in part of the story • the story does not have a satisfying conclusion	• events are out of order and hard to follow • dialogue and illustrations are not used • the story does not have a conclusion

Expert Model

Features of Poetry

Poetry is different from other forms of writing. It's a form that focuses on experiences, feelings, and ideas. A free-verse poem

- can have any number of lines and stanzas, which are grouped sets of lines
- does not always rhyme
- uses alliteration, onomatopoeia, metaphor, personification, and other types of figurative language

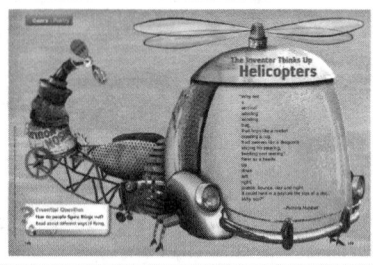

Literature Anthology: pages 148–149

Analyze an Expert Model Reread "The Inventor Thinks Up Helicopters" on page 149 in the **Literature Anthology**. Use text evidence to answer the questions below.

How does the poet use figurative language?

_____

_____

How does the poet's use of both long and short lines help to describe the movement of a helicopter?

_____

_____

Word Wise

On page 149, poet Patricia Hubbell uses onomatopoeia to make her poem appeal to your senses. *Whirling* means "quickly turning." When you say *whirling,* it sounds like what it means.

Plan: Choose Your Topic

COLLABORATE

Brainstorm With a partner, think about a time that you had to figure something out. Talk about a plan or invention and how it could solve a problem. Use these sentence starters.

The problem is . . .

A fun invention that would solve the problem is . . .

This invention would . . .

Writing Prompt Choose one of the plans or inventions to write a free-verse poem about.

I will write about _____

Purpose and Audience An author's purpose is the main reason for writing. Your audience is who will be reading your poem.

The reason I chose this topic is _____

_____

I want my audience to feel _____

_____

Quick Tip

When you write a poem, you are sharing your ideas. As you plan your poem, ask: *What do I want people to learn about my invention? What words, phrases, or rhythm patterns would best help me share my ideas?*

Freewrite In your writer's notebook, write as many ideas as you can think of about your invention. What problem does it solve? How did you think of it? What is most important about it? Write as many words as you can that will help you describe it.

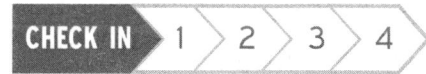
CHECK IN 1 2 3 4

Plan: Ideas

Ideas Poets use interesting words and details to bring their ideas to life and help readers paint a mental picture of what is being described in the poem.

Let's look at another expert model. Reread these lines from "Empanada Day."

> One bite of Abuelita's empanadas
> And my mouth purrs like a cat.

The word *purrs* is onomatopoeia, or a word that sounds like what it means. How does it help you understand how the speaker feels about empanadas?

_____

_____

_____

 **Plan** In your writer's notebook, draw a word web. Write the topic of your free-verse poem in the middle oval. Then write words that describe your ideas.

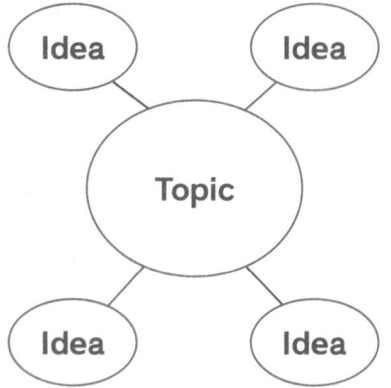

Idea — Idea — Topic — Idea — Idea

CHECK IN 1 2 3 4

Draft

Rhythm and Rhyme Poets use rhyme schemes, or patterns, to make poems sound musical. A free-verse poem might not rhyme, but it has a rhythm, or pattern formed by stressed syllables.

These two lines from "Empanada Day" rhyme. They also have the same rhythm. You can hear it by reading the lines aloud.

> "Teach me," I beg and bounce on my feet,
>
> "Teach me to make this magical treat."

Now use these two lines as a model to write about how you figured something out. Use rhyming words and rhythm.

_____

_____

_____

_____

Write a Draft Use your word web to write your draft in your writer's notebook. Choose words that make your poem musical and make your ideas come to life.

Quick Tip

Remember that a draft is just your first time writing. Don't worry about making everything perfect. You will have time to fix any mistakes later. Just try to get all your ideas written down.

CHECK IN 1 > 2 > 3 > 4

WRITING

Revise

Figurative Language Poets often use figurative language, such as metaphor, personification, alliteration, and onomatopoeia. Figurative language can make a poem more interesting to read. It helps readers better visualize what is happening in a poem.

Read the poem below. Think about words and phrases you can add to make it more interesting to read. Then revise the poem by adding figurative language.

Quick Tip

A metaphor compares two things without *like* or *as*: *The stars were diamonds in the sky.* Personification is when a writer gives a human action or quality to an object: *The tall grass whispered in the wind.*

> My sneakers take me all over town.
>
> We go up and down hills, jump across puddles.
>
> I've had these sneakers a very long time.

_____

_____

_____

_____

 **Revise** Revise your draft. Make sure you choose words that help readers picture your ideas. Look for lines you can rewrite to include figurative language.

CHECK IN 1 2 3 4

Peer Conferences

COLLABORATE

Review a Draft Listen carefully as your partner reads his or her draft aloud. Say what you like about the draft. Use these sentence starters to discuss your partner's draft.

I like this part of the poem because I could see . . .

Can you use rhyme or rhythm here to . . .

Use more figurative language to help me picture . . .

Partner Feedback After you take turns giving each other feedback, write one of the suggestions from your partner that you will use in your revision.

_____

_____

_____

_____

_____

_____

Revision After you finish your peer conference, use the Revising Checklist to figure out what you can change to make your poem better. Remember to use the rubric on page 215.

Revising Checklist

☐ Are my ideas clearly described?

☐ Did I use figurative language?

☐ Is there rhyme and/ or rhythm in my poem?

☐ Did I choose words that are funny and memorable?

Tech Tip

Word processing programs will give you the choice of using different fonts, or letter styles. This useful tool can make your writing more descriptive and interesting to read.

Edit and Proofread

When you edit and proofread your writing, you look for and correct mistakes in grammar, spelling, and punctuation. Read your draft at least three times. This will help you catch any mistakes. Use the checklist below to edit your poem.

Editing Checklist

- ☐ Do all lines begin with a capital letter?
- ☐ Is there punctuation at the end of every sentence?
- ☐ Are there apostrophes in possessive nouns?
- ☐ Are all words spelled correctly?

List two mistakes that you found as you proofread your poem.

1 _____

_____

_____

2 _____

_____

_____

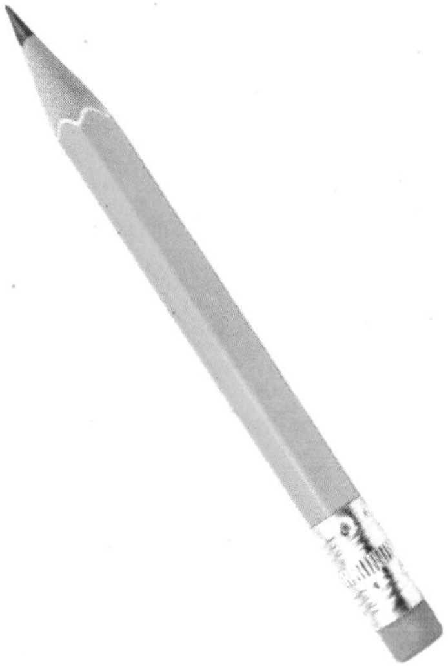

Grammar Connections

When you proofread your draft for punctuation mistakes, remember to use an apostrophe to show possession. For example, "My sister's sneakers are bright blue."

Publish, Present, and Evaluate

Publishing When you publish your writing, you create a neat final copy that is free of mistakes. If you are not using a computer, use your best handwriting. Write legibly in print or cursive.

Presentation When you are ready to present, practice your presentation. Use the Presenting Checklist.

Evaluate After you publish, use the rubric to evaluate your poem.

What did you do successfully? _____

_____

What needs more work? _____

_____

✓ **Presenting Checklist**

☐ Look at your audience.

☐ Speak loudly and clearly.

☐ Use expression to convey the mood of your poem.

☐ Pause at the end of lines or phrases.

Turn to page 199. Fill in the bars to show what you learned.

4	3	2	1
• excellent use of figurative language; descriptions are vivid • excellent use of rhyme and rhythm; writing is smooth and fun to read • includes correct spelling and grammar	• good use of figurative language; descriptions are clear • good use of rhyme and rhythm; writing sounds like poetry • has a spelling or grammar error	• some use of figurative language; descriptions are somewhat unclear • some use of rhyme and rhythm; writing is choppy in places • has several spelling or grammar errors	• no use of figurative language; descriptions are unclear • no use of rhyme or rhythm; writing is difficult to understand • has frequent spelling or grammar errors

TAKE NOTES

Take notes and annotate as you read the passages "Lighting with Less" and "Someday."

Look for the answer to the question. *How do people find creative solutions to problems?*

_____

_____

_____

_____

_____

_____

_____

PASSAGE 1

EXPOSITORY TEXT

Lighting with

Most people need light at night to read or work. But not everyone can afford power stations in their towns. Inventors have found ways to produce light for pennies a day. Here are some of their ideas for producing light with less.

Old Light Tricks

Before electric lights were invented, people put metal pans behind candles or gas lights. This made them look brighter. To get a bright work light, they set a bottle of water near a window or a candle. The bottle acted like a lens. It focused light on a single spot.

Light from Motion

A dynamo is a simple tool. It turns energy from things that move into electricity. A small dynamo moved by the wind, a waterwheel, or a bike can make enough electricity to power a light. A battery can store the electricity for use later. You do have to buy a dynamo and battery, but then the electricity is free.

Light Weight

Weighted lights use gravity to get power. To start it, a weight is attached to one end of a chain. The weight slowly pulls a wheel around inside the light. That spins a dynamo, which makes electricity to light a light bulb.

Sunlight at Night

Solar lanterns don't cost much. They can shine all night. A solar panel on top of the light charges its battery during the day. At night, the battery powers an LED light. Once you've bought the lamp, there is no extra cost for electricity.

PASSAGE 2   REALISTIC FICTION

Someday

Someday I am going to be a great inventor. But for now, I have to get to school.

I'm almost out the door when my brother calls, "Hey Ada, we have to put away the blocks!" Rats! We were supposed to do it last night. Someday, I'm going to invent a block picking-up robot that will sort all the pieces by color and type. It will be so cool!

"OK, but let's hurry!" I say. As I open the closet door, an empty shoe holder swings back and forth. That gives me an idea . . .

TAKE NOTES

TAKE NOTES

_____

_____

_____

_____

_____

_____

_____

_____

_____

_____

_____

_____

_____

"Hey, we can put them in this!" There's a pocket for each size block. Good enough until I can build my robot.

"Argh!" As I'm zipping up my coat, the zipper pull breaks off! There's just a little hole that I can't grab. I need something like a hook. Or a bendy wire, like . . . a paper clip! I grab one from the desk, bend the end, and slip it through the hole. Zip!

Outside everything is covered in ice, and I slip a bit on the stairs. My fuzzy mitten sticks to the icy railing. How silly is that! Mittens stick to ice, but shoes slip! But the mitten gives me an idea. I go back inside and get an old pair of my dad's socks. I put them on over my shoes. It looks a bit funny, but I don't slip!

During lunchtime at school, my friend Fiona wants to share her jam roll. Yum! But how can we cut it? No one has a knife. What we need, I think, is a mini laser cutter that can cut anything into any shape. While I'm thinking about that, I remember that I have some dental floss in my lunch box. Mom says it's important that I floss after eating. I tie the floss around the jam roll and pull the ends tight. Ta-da! It cuts the jam roll pretty well, but not as well as a laser, of course.

I think I may already be a great inventor!

COMPARE THE PASSAGES

Review your notes from "Lighting with Less" and "Someday."
Create a Venn diagram. Use your notes and the diagram to write
how what you learned in the two passages is alike and different.

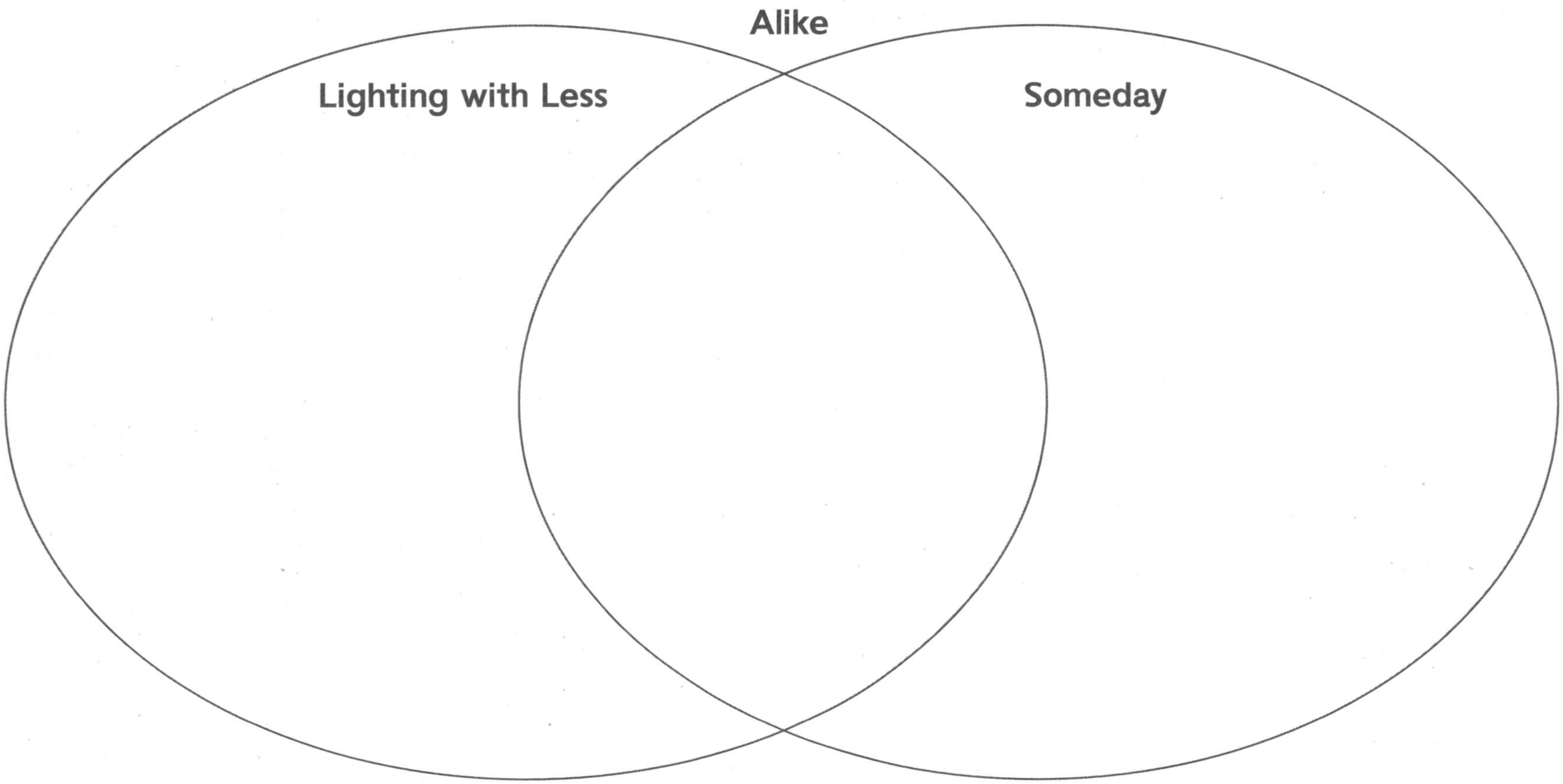

Alike

Lighting with Less

Someday

Synthesize Information

Think about both texts. What everyday item could you use in a
new way to solve a problem? How would you use it?

CHECK IN 1 2 3 4

LIGHT MOVES

A beam of light will travel in a straight line. When light hits an object, the light can either **reflect**, **refract**, or **absorb**. You can explore each of the ways light moves.

Gather up the materials: flashlight, mirror, glass of water, pencil, black construction paper.

Reflect: Light bounces off a surface. Shine a flashlight into a mirror. The light will bounce off the shiny surface. Try it!

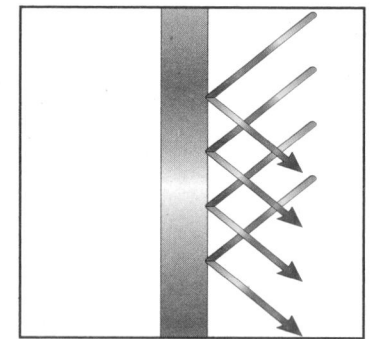 

Refract: Light goes through an object and bends. Put a pencil in a glass of water. Light bends around the pencil and makes it look broken. Try it!

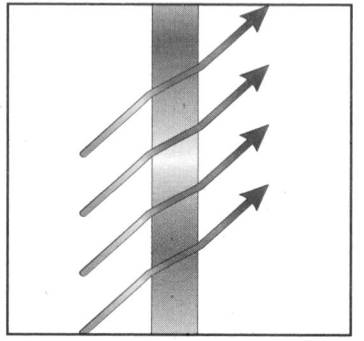 

Absorb: Light stops and does not reflect (bounce) or refract (bend). Light is transformed or changed into heat. Use a flashlight and focus the beam onto a piece of black construction paper. Wait a few minutes. Touch the paper. How does it feel?

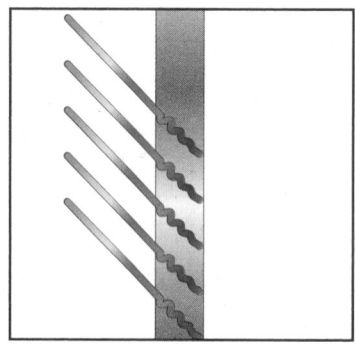 

(tl, cl, bl)Fouad A. Saad/Shutterstock, (tr)Ken Karp/McGraw-Hill Education, (cr)patrickhastings/123RF, (br)New Africa/Shutterstock

EXPLORING HOW LIGHT MOVES

Experiment with light and objects around you. First predict if the light will reflect or absorb. Then test the object by shining a flashlight on it. Then record your observations.

Gather up the materials: flashlight, mirror, aluminum foil, three objects of your choice (make your own chart for these).

Object	Prediction	Observation
mirror		
aluminum foil		

LAB REPORT

Use your light experiment results to write a lab report.

Question: What happens when you shine a light on objects?

_____

_____

Write a statement about light using the terms *reflect* and *absorb*.

_____

_____

My Goal I can read and understand social studies texts.

TAKE NOTES

Take notes and annotate as you read the passages "Solving Local Problems" and "What Constitutes a Constitution?"

Look for the answer to the question. *How does the local government help solve problems?*

_____

_____

_____

_____

_____

_____

_____

PASSAGE 1

EXPOSITORY TEXT

Solving Local Problems

If you have a problem at home, you ask an adult for help. If you have a problem at school, you ask your teacher for help. But what if you have a problem in your community? Whom would you turn to for help?

Local Leaders

Local governments take care of issues in cities or towns. A state's constitution often determines how local governments are set up.

In many cities and towns, a mayor is the leader of the local government. The people elect their mayor by voting. Other cities and towns might have a city manager. A city manager is not elected, but instead is appointed by the state government.

Mayors do not work alone. There is usually a group of people, called a city council, who work with the mayor. Together they make important decisions and solve problems. The members of the city council are elected by people.

The mayor and city council members work together with police officers, firefighters, and park managers.

Dave and Les Jacobs/Blend Images/Getty Images

Solving Problems

Local governments deal with many kinds of public issues. They deal with anything from street signs and roads, to parks and schools, to trash and sewers.

When citizens have a concern in their community, they can go to their local government. For example, someone might want a stop sign put on a corner near her home. She might think that people drive too fast. Or a person might want his street repaved because it has big holes.

There are many ways to tell your local government about a problem. City councils hold meetings that are open to citizens. They can attend to listen and voice concerns. The mayor and city council then look into problems and reach a solution. Citizens can write letters to their government. And many local governments have websites where citizens can get information and contact the mayor or city council.

Local governments are a great resource for citizens. Find out who is part of your local government. That way, if you have a problem, you'll know whom to contact.

TAKE NOTES

TAKE NOTES

_____

_____

_____

_____

_____

_____

_____

_____

_____

_____

_____

_____

_____

PASSAGE 2 · EXPOSITORY TEXT

WHAT CONSTITUTES A CONSTITUTION?

What is a constitution? The word has two meanings. The first is a body of laws that a group agrees to follow. The second is "the formation" of something. When the founders formed our constitution, they also formed our nation. The Constitution is the supreme, or most important, law of the land. Everyone must follow the Constitution's laws.

The U.S. Constitution is how our nation's government works. But each state also has their own constitution.

A state constitution tells who the people are that run the state government. For instance, the person in charge of the state is the governor. The state constitution must follow the rules of the U.S. Constitution. But a state constitution allows for laws that are special for that state. For instance, the Florida Constitution has special rules about the Everglades.

For a country, state, or town government to run smoothly, we must all agree on the laws. A national or state constitution ensures that everyone follows the same rules. A constitution protects everyone's rights and does so fairly. That's what constitutes a constitution!

©Tetra Images/CORBIS

COMPARE THE PASSAGES

Review your notes from "Solving Local Problems" and "What Constitutes a Constitution?" Make a Venn diagram. Use your notes to tell how information in the two passages is alike and different.

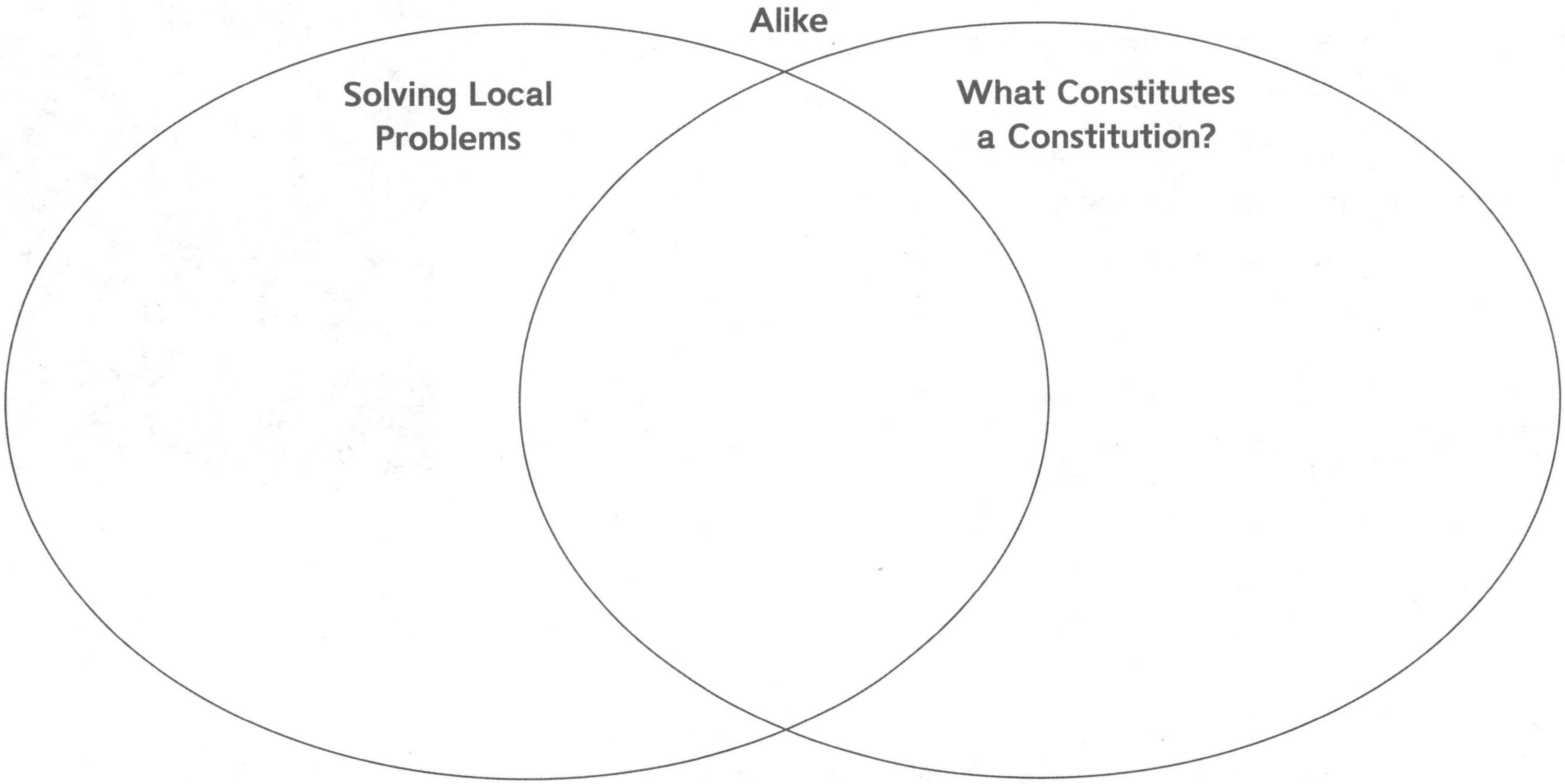

Alike

Solving Local
Problems

What Constitutes
a Constitution?

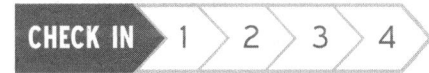

Synthesize Information

Think about both texts. Why do you think towns, cities, and states need their own constitutions?

CHECK IN 1 2 3 4

CLASSROOM CONSTITUTION

You've read about constitutions. Now it's time to create a constitution for your classroom. Think about the rules you will include and what they will do to help keep your classroom running smoothly.

Some rules you might want to put into your Classroom Constitution might be:

- one person talks at a time
- no mean words or name-calling
- eyes on the person who is talking

Work in a group and name three rules for your class.

1. _____

2. _____

3. _____

Make a poster explaining your rules and present them to the class. After everyone has presented their rules, the class can vote on their top three rules.

Once your classroom has voted, work with your class to create a Classroom Constitution bulletin board and post the class rules.

Reflect on Your Learning

Talk About It Reflect on what you learned in this unit. Then talk with a partner about how you did.

I am really proud of how I can _____

_____

_____

_____

Something I need to work more on is _____

_____

_____

_____

Share a goal you have with a partner.

My Goal Set a goal for Unit 3. In your reader's notebook, write about what you can do to get there.